I'D EAT THAT!

SIMPLE WAYS TO BE A BETTER COOK

I'D EAT THAT!

SIMPLE WAYS TO BE A BETTER COOK

CALLUM HANN

MURDOCH BOOKS

CONTENTS

INTRODUCTION

My dad had two pieces of advice for me when it came to working: 'Get a job you actually enjoy,' he would say. Check. And 'don't ever start your own business' (like he and Mum did), as 'it's bloody hard work'. Whoops! Sorry Dad. One out of two isn't bad!

What a fantastic eighteen months it's been since the first *Starter Kitchen* book hit the shelves. Between starting Sprout, my own cooking school with dietitian Themis Chryssidis; designing a range of food products with the Thankyou™ team; working with Adelaide Produce Market, Wesley Mission, Chef de Quota, Jamie Oliver's Home Cooking Skills and Connect Pink; becoming a presenter on *SA Life* and winning $20,000 for the Cancer Council on *MasterChef All Stars*, I've had my hands full!

The sources of inspiration for the recipes in this book are varied. I grew up eating mostly Australian/European and vegetarian-style dishes, so some of these recipes are things I ate as a child. A few are from friends and others were discovered on my travels. You may notice I've lifted many of the recipe ideas from countries outside Australia, most noticeably North America, South Africa and parts of Asia. These are the places I've been lucky enough to travel to during my twenty-four years. As food is such a universal language, I find meeting new people from different cultures to be incredibly inspiring in the kitchen.

I've also been lucky to learn from friends and family. There are various Asian recipes from Adam, burgers from Dan and Rob, vegetarian food (where you don't even miss the meat!) from my sister, Kirsty, and a comforting chilli from Kyle (page 102). I have learned about precision, baking and how to make a darn fine salted caramel popcorn fudge (page 62) from Chloe, who now owns four sets of measuring cups if that gives you an idea of the sort of person she is. Technically, I melted one of the sets, but that's a story for another day …

I'm always looking for shortcuts in recipes, whether it's the potato-free gnocchi (page 91) or the sort-of paella (page 66) made with couscous instead of rice. Some would call me a lazy cook, but I prefer the word efficient (I was an engineering student prior to becoming a cook). Don't get me wrong, I love cooking, but if you can get a delicious meal on the table that is quicker and easier to prepare than the original recipe, yet sacrifices nothing in terms of taste or enjoyment, which would you choose?

The average person has about nine different recipes in their repertoire that they cook over and over again. Nine meals?! That doesn't sound like a heck of a lot of variety to me. I hope this collection of recipes you hold in your hands gives you the skills and, more importantly, the enthusiasm to become a better cook. Even if you only pick up an extra handful of recipes that you like and want to make again, you can sit above that average and eat a greater variety of meals.

My goal is to turn you into more of a foodie than you already are. Feel free to change, bastardise, scribble on, leave stuff out of or add to my recipes. This book isn't about me, it's about you. I want you to become a better cook, a more knowledgeable cook, and a happier cook. Try something new. If the worst thing about today is a lopsided soufflé, then that sounds like a pretty darn good day to me. Cook dishes for no other reason than to make yourself and others happy. That'll make me happy. I'll be around for dinner next week!

TIPS TO HELP YOU BECOME A BETTER COOK

THE OVERARCHING PRINCIPLES OF BECOMING A BETTER COOK

I'm always learning about food, but here is some of the best advice I've been given.

- No matter how good a cook you are, you can't disguise crap ingredients. Good-quality ingredients = good food. See my section on fruit, vegetables and seasonality (page 16).
- Don't be too serious about food. If you're not having fun, what's the point? Do get serious about where your food comes from. Please buy free-range eggs, if for no other reason than if you were a chicken, you'd want a little wing-flapping room. Buy food from your country or state where possible. Give a damn about the planet.
- Simple is often best. If in doubt, less is more. This applies both to individual dishes and to whole menus.
- You don't necessarily need years of culinary training to be a good cook. If you eat good food, read cookbooks, try new things and expand your repertoire, you can be a great cook.
- Work cleanly. Clean in the kitchen as you go so you don't end up with a big pile of washing-up at the end. Clean cook = clean food. This is a tip I've ignored for most of my life but have realised the importance of recently.
- You don't need a million kitchen gadgets. A sharp knife, a sturdy chopping board and a decent frying pan will allow you to cook unlimited great meals. Oh, and make sure you have a wire balloon whisk. Whisks with plastic or silicone bits on the end just don't whip things properly.
- Be respectful of what others teach you in the kitchen. There is rarely only one right way to do something, so be open-minded to learning. A pastry chef I know has over thirty different chocolate mousse recipes filed away. He collects them every time he works or travels in search of the perfect mousse!
- Figure out what kind of food you like best, and cook that.
- And finally, master the basics. So much good food is created when basic techniques are performed well.

TIPS FOR ENTERTAINING AT HOME

Having mates over for dinner? Want to impress your girlfriend's parents? Here's my advice for making the occasion as stress-free as possible:

- Serving simple food and being able to enjoy yourself is always better than serving complex food while you're running around like a headless chicken!
- If you're serving more than one course, try and cook as much of the food as possible the day before or the morning of the meal. For example, making a passionfruit parfait (page 153) the night before will leave you with one less job to do on the night.
- Strategically pick dishes that are made using different areas of the kitchen: an oven dish, a stovetop dish, and a dessert that sets in the fridge, for example. This ensures you won't run out of space.
- If you are eating outside, have sunblock on hand if it's during the day and mozzie repellent at night.
- Make your life easier by serving platters of food for people to help themselves rather than putting food onto individual plates.
- Ask your guests if they have any dietary requirements, allergies or if they can't stand a particular food before you decide on the menu. You don't need to go to the effort of asking if they like olives or not, but you don't want to serve a seafood banquet to someone who only eats red meat, or pasta to a gluten-intolerant friend.
- If there's left-over food, try and use it up in the next night's dinner. Cooked meat can be topped with pastry and baked for a quick pie, and roast veggies heated and blended with a little chicken stock make a quick soup.
- If you're serving alcohol, also have a funky mocktail on standby to make sure drivers and underage folk feel included.
- Don't think that it's your responsibility to do everything; you want to make sure you're having as much fun as your friends! Most people will be more than happy to help out if you ask.

FRUIT, VEGETABLES & SEASONALITY

WHY BUY FRUIT & VEGETABLES IN SEASON?

The food you cook can only ever be as good as the ingredients you use. Once upon a time you could only buy fruit and vegetables in season. Now, with different farming techniques and people transporting food all over the world, we can pretty much get anything at any time of the year. While this is convenient, I'm going to try and convince you that it's worth learning a bit more about seasonality and what to cook, when.

COST

Foods that are in season cost less. It's basically supply and demand; fruit and vegetables grown and picked in their natural season are easy for farmers to grow, so they often end up with a glut. This means seasonal produce should be plentiful and easy to find. When things are plentiful, they usually cost less, which is great for your wallet! Similarly, supermarkets don't need to bump up their prices to pay for transportation costs of produce coming from overseas when it comes from local areas.

TASTE

Food allowed to ripen properly in natural conditions simply tastes better than something that's been in the cargo hold of a plane. If you don't believe me, eat a tomato in summer and a tomato in winter and compare the two.

HEALTH

Fruit and vegetables get all their nutrients from the soil they are grown in and are at their nutritional peak when ripe. This also means that the roots of fruit and veg tend to be the most vitamin- and mineral-dense (so eat your broccoli stems!). When a product is transported a long distance, it is picked early and allowed to ripen en route to its next destination. So fruit and vegetables may change colour in a truck on the way to a supermarket, but they won't develop nutritionally. Also, by eating an array of different fruits and vegetables throughout the year as they come into season, you are ensuring you are getting a greater range of nutrients.

ENVIRONMENTAL CONSIDERATIONS

When food is imported from all corners of the globe to ensure that we can access the same fruit and veg all year round, a significant carbon footprint is created. Eating seasonal food not only supports your local industry, it's better for the environment, too.

WHAT'S IN SEASON, WHEN?

Here is a seasonal chart to help you find cheap, great-looking produce in every season (it has an Aussie bias, but if you live elsewhere just track down a chart to suit your area). Most produce isn't just in season for a few months of the year; many types of fruit and veg overlap several seasons. However, this is a good guide if you're not sure what to have for dinner. Whichever season you're in, have a look at this list and find what you love. Build your meal around a couple of 'in-season ingredients'.

SUMMER

Tomatoes, zucchini (courgettes), eggplants (aubergines), chillies, beans, capsicums (peppers), cucumbers, cabbages, celery, sweetcorn, peaches, nectarines, apricots, plums, blueberries, raspberries, blackberries, strawberries, watermelons, honeydew melons, rockmelons, passionfruit, lettuces, cherries, grapes, lychees, mangoes.

AUTUMN

Pumpkins (winter squash), figs, pomegranates, apples, pears, kiwi fruit, lemons, persimmons, quince, beetroots (beets), mushrooms and wild mushrooms, broccoli, brussels sprouts, celery, sweetcorn, grapes, beans, turnips, cabbages, carrots, lettuces, parsnips, snow peas (mangetout), sugarsnap peas, zucchini (courgettes), spinach.

WINTER

Sweet potatoes, swedes, celeriacs, leeks, pumpkins (winter squash), cauliflowers, cabbages, Asian greens, globe artichokes, Jerusalem artichokes, lemons, apples, oranges, grapefruit, tamarillos, kiwi fruit, Chinese cabbages (wongboks), fennel, radicchio, spinach.

SPRING

Asparagus, peas, beans, snow peas (mangetout), broad beans, strawberries, spring onions (scallions), leeks, fennel, witlof (chicory), grapefruit, lemons, oranges, papayas (sometimes called paw paws), cabbages, rhubarb, silverbeet (Swiss chard).

MY GUIDE TO COOKING FISH

Fish is incredibly versatile, simple to cook, good for you and delicious. However, many people I meet are a little bit wary about cooking it: scared of over- or undercooking it, which method to use for which fish, which fish to use when ... Ironically, one of the most commonly cooked proteins is chicken breast, which I think is far more unforgiving when undercooked and horribly dry and stringy when overcooked. So, if you can cook chicken, you can cook seafood!

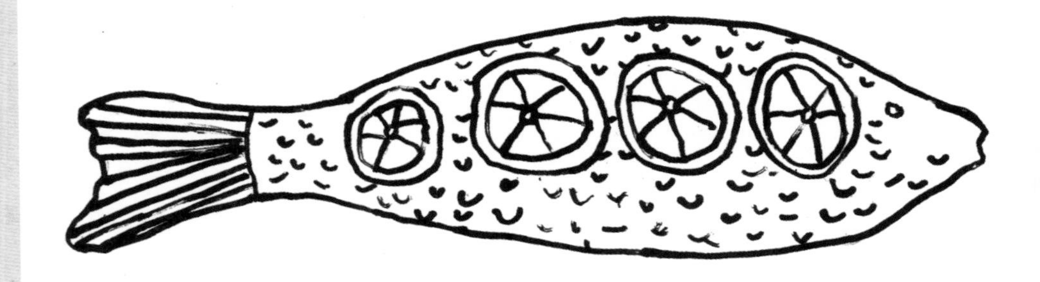

HOW TO TELL IF FISH IS COOKED

Knowing when fish is cooked is no more difficult than testing a cake. A skewer inserted into cooked fish will slide in easily, but will meet resistance when inserted into uncooked flesh. Another way to test is by pressing the fish with a spoon or tongs; if it flakes apart, it is cooked, if it still seems quite firm, cook it a little longer. Visually, fish will turn opaque as it cooks. Remember that, like a steak, fish doesn't necessarily need to be cooked all the way through. Tuna and salmon both benefit from being a little under (or rare) in the middle.

WHICH FISH, WHEN?

There are many different varieties of fish you can find at a fishmonger, supermarket or on the end of your line. The great thing about fish is that if a recipe calls for a specific type of fish, you can generally substitute it with another similar-looking one. As a general rule, white fish of a similar thickness are interchangeable and ocean trout makes a great alternative to salmon. Thin fish will cook in a couple of minutes on each side in a frying pan, under a grill (broiler) or on a barbecue. If you cook a whole fish or particularly thick fillets, oven-baked is a good way to go. I like to buy fish from a fishmonger because you can always ask them questions if in doubt and they'll be happy to help.

HOW DO I COOK FISH?

There are several different ways you can cook your fish.

PAN-FRYING

This is one of my favourite methods, as the skin becomes crisp and the cooking time is short. Get your pan hot enough so it'll sizzle, add a glug of canola, rice bran or vegetable oil (not olive oil as it will smoke in a really hot pan) then add your fish, skin side down. The fish will immediately retract and shrink slightly upon contact with the pan, so it's best to hold the fish in the pan fairly firmly for 10–15 seconds with a spatula, egg slide or your hand. This ensures the fish keeps its shape, and that the skin has the largest possible surface area to get crispy. Cook the fish for the majority of the time on the skin side, as it means crisper skin and it also helps to keep the fish moist. If this floats your boat, check out my Cajun fish with sweetcorn, red onion and smoked almond salad on page 92. If the fish you are cooking is really thin (1.5 cm/½ inch or under), you may not need to flip it over at all.

STEAMING

Flavour-wise, steaming doesn't really add much to your fish, so make sure you include some seasoning, herbs or spices. This cooking method does give your fish a fantastic soft, moist texture. If your fish has the skin on, it's best to peel or slice it off before cooking. Steaming is a super-quick way to cook and you can steam veggies at the same time for an easy meal.

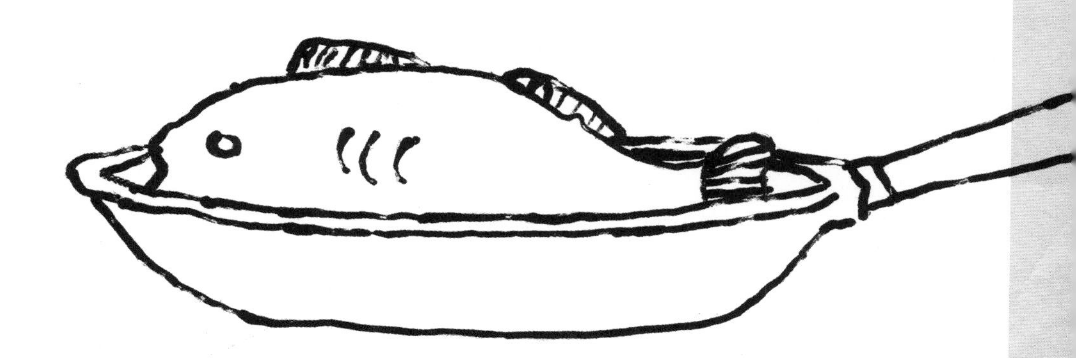

GRILLING (BROILING)

Particularly useful with thin fillets, grilling is a fairly direct form of heat but less aggressive than pan-frying. I like to use this method for fish that has had the skin removed. Place your fish on a tray, give it a little drizzle of oil, a pinch of salt and a scattering of some herbs and spices before placing it under the grill. The fish will take between 2–5 minutes to cook this way, depending on the thickness of the fillets you're cooking.

POACHING

Like steaming, poached fish provides great texture, but the more flavour you can add to the cooking liquid the better off your fish will be. Thin, brothy liquids such as water or stock can benefit from some lemon slices, parsley stalks or peppercorns. My favourite way to poach fish, though, is to do it in a richer sauce such as tomato or curry. Importantly, you must never boil the fish as it will make it dry; cook it at a very gentle temperature.

DEEP-FRYING

Deep-fried fish has a super-crunchy outside and a very tender, steamed inside. It is best to coat the fish in a batter, crumb or seasoned flour to insulate and flavour the flesh. Thin, white fish fillets tend to be best suited for deep-frying. Ensure the oil is nice and hot (about 180°C/350°F) before you add the fish so it cooks quickly and doesn't soak up too much oil. Deep-fried fish will cook very quickly (sometimes in a matter of seconds!) so keep an eye on it as it cooks.

BAKING

This is a technique often saved for whole fish, where an even, slower cooking technique is required. Stuff the fish with aromatic ingredients such as fennel, garlic, citrus and herbs before transferring to the oven.

COOKING IN A BAG (EN PAPILLOTE)

Somewhere between baking and steaming, cooking in a bag is a great way to cook fish if you're a bit unsure. It's a very forgiving technique and any flavours you seal in the bag will really penetrate into the fish. Check out the recipes on pages 136 and 137 for more on this technique.

HARMONIOUS FLAVOUR COMBINATIONS

I'm sure there are times when you follow a recipe to a T, other times you customise it to your own taste, and then occasions when you might make it up completely. I've put together a handy guide to flavours that work well with each other, so if you're ever staring into your fridge wondering what you might serve with that piece of leftover pork, you can find inspiration here.

INGREDIENTS THAT LOVE CHICKEN

- Herbs like parsley, tarragon, coriander (cilantro), chives, thyme and rosemary.
- Vegetables such as carrots, celery, potato, pumpkin (winter squash), leek, mushrooms, fennel, Asian greens and peas.
- Chicken loves being cooked with, or wrapped in, salty ingredients; bacon or olives work perfectly.
- Acidic ingredients like citrus fruits and yoghurt are also nice added towards the end of the cooking time in chicken dishes.

INGREDIENTS THAT LOVE LAMB

- Herbs like thyme, oregano, mint and rosemary. (Don't buy rosemary! I guarantee someone you know has a big bush of it in their garden.)
- Vegetables such as asparagus, green beans, zucchini (courgettes), parsnips, carrots and peas.
- Salty ingredients like olives and anchovies work brilliantly with lamb, as do sweet ingredients such as currants, pomegranates and honey.

INGREDIENTS THAT LOVE FISH & SEAFOOD

- Herbs like coriander (cilantro), chives, parsley, thyme and oregano.
- Vegetables like celery, fennel, leek, leafy greens, cucumber, broccoli and tomatoes.
- The flavours of aromatic ingredients penetrate beautifully into fish. Try lemongrass, lime leaves, star anise, citrus fruits, ginger, garlic, white pepper and dill.

INGREDIENTS THAT LOVE BEEF

- Herbs such as thyme, tarragon, coriander (cilantro) and parsley.
- Vegetables such as chillies, potato, pumpkin (winter squash), tomatoes dark leafy greens, mushrooms and onion.
- Other hero ingredients such as red wine, bacon, horseradish, mustard and black pepper are perfect for bringing out the best in a beef dish.

INGREDIENTS THAT LOVE PORK

- Herbs like sage, rosemary and thyme.
- Vegetables such as fennel, cabbage, celery, radishes, parsnips, tomatoes, Asian greens and bitter leaves.
- Cider and dry white wine are both great ingredients for pork recipes needing a splash of liquid.
- Spices like cinnamon, star anise and fennel seeds love pork.
- And for a hint of sweetness, pork also loves all types of fruit: apples, pears, figs and cherries all cut through rich pork dishes beautifully.

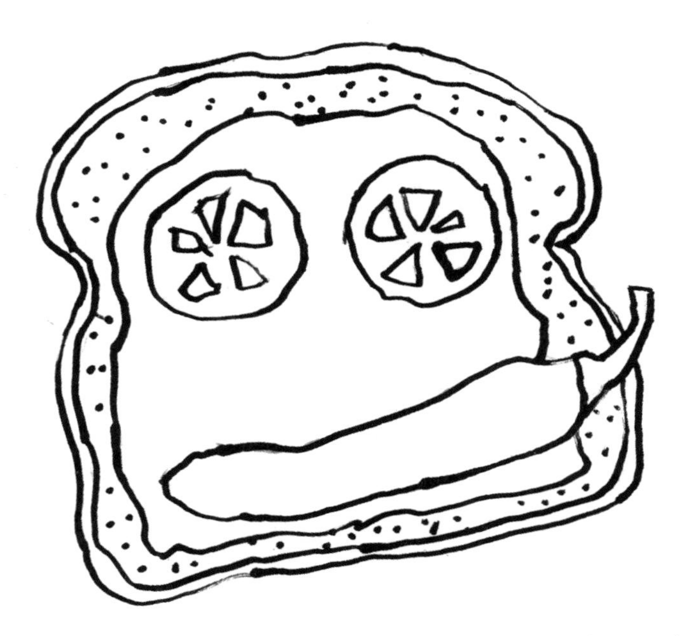

This whole harmonious flavours thing leads me nicely onto this next bit:

SO, YOU WANT TO CREATE YOUR OWN RECIPES?

Awesome. Good cooks follow recipes to a T for delicious results; great cooks start to alter recipes to their own preferences and, in time, write their own recipes. I want you to become a great cook. We are at such an exciting time for sharing recipes with blogs, food websites, books, magazines and e-books being just some of the mediums we have available to us. I'm hoping that between recipe ideas from this book, the harmonious flavour combinations I've suggested and the tips I'm about to give you, you'll be able to invent and write some of your own recipes.

Before I was lucky enough to be given the opportunity to write cookbooks, I loved being able to type up a recipe and give it to a friend to try. Similarly, I would try and get recipes from friends and family to constantly be expanding my cooking repertoire. Who knows, maybe I'll be reading your cookbook in a few years' time!

HOW TO GET YOUR CREATIVE SIDE BREWING FOR YOUR OWN RECIPE IDEAS

There are several ways to get inspiration for a recipe. Here are my three favourites:

1. Start with your favourite cuisine in mind. If you love French food, start by thinking of existing French dishes and flavours and a way you could combine some of your own favourite ingredients. Look at the classic techniques of that cuisine. Indian dishes tend to be cooked slowly in liquid to allow flavours to develop; South-East Asian dishes are often about quickly cooked meals packed with sweet, salty and sour ingredients. Italian cooking is well known for using a few hero ingredients and really making them shine. The list goes on.

2. Start with a hero ingredient. It can be a type of meat, or a fruit or vegetable that's in season. Once you have your hero ingredient in mind, think about which cooking technique you want to use. Do you want to stew or braise it slowly with lots of spices and hard herbs? Do you want to cook it super-quickly in a pan? Is oven-roasting a good way to bring out its best flavour? Once you know what you want to cook, and how you want to cook it, think of other ingredients that will complement your hero ingredient in terms of both flavour and texture. The section on pages 24 and 25 is a useful tool if you need some inspiration.

3. Look at what you have in your fridge and pantry and try to make the best dish you can. Remember that less is often more; don't overcomplicate things just for the sake of it. This is a challenge that many of us face every day at dinnertime, but I promise it's a great creative tool.

CONTRAST, CONTRAST, CONTRAST!

When you are adding additional ingredients to a recipe, keep in mind that it's desirable to have a balance of flavours, textures and colours. This ensures that every bite of a meal, from the first to the last, is interesting and different. For example, lots of people add avocado to a salad; I think it's so popular due to its soft, creamy texture alongside crisp vegetables. Similarly, a squeeze of lemon for acidity or some fresh herbs added at the end of a rich dish can lighten up the flavours and make all the difference.

OK, SO NOW YOU KNOW WHAT YOU WANT TO COOK. HOW DO YOU WRITE THE RECIPE?

I think it is always best to write the recipe before you start cooking, so you can adjust and correct quantities and steps as you cook. If you just cook a dish and think you'll remember everything to write down afterwards, you'll never get the same accuracy level or detail. Everyone has their own recipe-writing style, but there are some golden rules to follow to make it easy for other people to understand and cook your dish. No matter how great the recipe is, if it's not user-friendly, people won't want to cook it.

MY GUIDELINES FOR WRITING A RECIPE

- List ingredients in the order they are used.
- Make sure all the ingredients in the method are listed, and all listed ingredients are used in the method!
- In the method, make sure steps like marinating, preheating ovens and lining baking trays are listed first.
- Cooking times are often approximate, so try and provide a gauge of what the food should look like. For example, 'roast chicken marylands for 35–40 minutes, or until golden brown and the juices run clear'.
- Be consistent with your measurements where possible. Try not to have weights, volumes, cup and spoon measurements all in the ingredients list together. However, if you are using cup measurements, ingredients that don't really fit into a cup that well, such as cold butter, are acceptable to list by weight.
- Be specific. Be aware that ½ a cup of chopped walnuts and ½ a cup of walnuts that are then chopped are not the same thing. Also, don't say 'a tin of coconut milk' as product sizes vary from brand to brand. Saying '1 x 400 g (14 oz) tin of coconut milk' is much better. Keep in mind that many ingredients come in different forms; peaches can be tinned, fresh or frozen, so if your recipe calls for peaches, specify which type to use.

- A recipe has to be practical. For example, a tin of condensed milk usually weighs 395 g (just under 14 oz), so if your recipe calls for 410 g of condensed milk, it is annoying for the reader to have to buy two tins and waste most of one of them.
- Specify equipment. Don't just say 'line a cake tin'. A cake will cook considerably differently in an 18 cm (7 inch) tin compared to a 22 cm (8½ inch) tin.
- Keep abbreviations consistent. If you call a tablespoon a tbsp, make sure you always write it this way to avoid confusion.
- Don't assume too much, and try to provide visual cues where possible. Rather than saying 'cream butter and sugar', say 'cream butter and sugar until light and fluffy'.
- Include warnings about the recipe if needed, such as 'Don't boil the heck out of the chicken when poaching, turn the water down and let it simmer gently.'
- For dessert and baking recipes accuracy is often crucial, so ingredients are usually specified in grams or cup measurements. Savoury recipes are usually taste-driven, so 'a large handful of bean sprouts' may be an acceptable measurement.

Good luck!

HOW TO HAVE A GREAT RESTAURANT EXPERIENCE

Even the most devoted home cooks love to go out for dinner sometimes. If you've got the night off from cooking and have some spare cash to burn on an awesome meal, check out my restaurant tips. I've included how to make sure you have a great experience, and how to avoid a lemon.

BEFORE YOU ARRIVE

- Keep in mind that the best places to eat are the ones with a particular focus or theme that they do darn well. Places that do a bit of everything tend to be pretty average.
- Look for places that have a menu that changes with the seasons. If they are serving asparagus or peaches all year round, they'll either be crap six months of the year, or you'll pay through the nose.
- Jump onto the restaurant's website and have a look at the menu before you go to see if it sounds like your sort of food.
- Use websites and blog reviews as a guideline, but take them with a pinch of salt. Whether other diners loved it or hated it might not reflect your opinion as everyone's experience at a restaurant is unique.
- Social media, such as Facebook and Twitter, is a great way to follow restaurants and see when they have a new menu or special. If you have a special dining request (such as dietary requirements) social media is a good way to interact and figure out if the place is right for you.

- Don't underestimate word-of-mouth. Ask your friends and family for recommendations. Similarly, if you have a great meal out, let your friends know.
- If you're eating in an unfamiliar city, try and eat where the locals are eating, not where there are only other tourists.
- Make sure you discuss where you want to eat with whoever you are dining with. I once took a friend to a place called Dumpling King not realising that he hated dumplings.
- If the restaurant takes bookings, make sure you book. If a restaurant doesn't take bookings, go out to eat early so you don't have to twiddle your thumbs waiting for a table to come up.
- A restaurant might have a great location or view, but that doesn't necessarily mean the food will be good. In fact, sometimes the food is overpriced rubbish that relies on the view to get people through the door. Having said that, this isn't a dealbreaker, just more of a guideline.

WHEN YOU GET THERE

- If the dining area looks dirty or is smelly, imagine what the kitchen looks like! I also think it's not a good sign if a restaurant has awful bathrooms.
- Be polite to the staff. If you are extra nice to them, they'll probably be extra nice to you. No one knows the food better than they do. If you're not sure what you want, ask what they would have if they were ordering.
- If you're eating in a pub, order what they do best: pub food. If not, don't be surprised when your crappy Thai curry isn't nearly as good as your friend's T-bone steak and chips.
- Great places make the extra effort. Are the staff dressed nicely? Are they friendly when they greet you? Is the menu well presented or old and tatty? Is the table set nicely and do the cutlery and glasses look clean and polished?
- Be aware of restaurants with enormous menus. How often do you think they turn over stock of their least popular dish? There are a few places with big menus that are great, but many can be a bit dodgy.
- If a dish looks out of place on a menu, don't order it. I know a great little Indian restaurant that does really tasty Indian food but, for some reason, has the most awful lasagne on the menu.
- If you have a great experience, let the staff know how much you loved it. People always pipe up when they have a complaint, but are often less vocal when it's good!

MORNING GLORY

What better way to start your day than with a pearler of a breakfast? With a big day ahead, I'm a bit of a muesli fan. If you're the same, give my pear and dried fig bircher muesli recipe (page 38) a go. On the weekends though, give me a cooked brekkie and a juice or coffee and I'm a happy guy. It's also a great way to entertain because breakfast and brunch recipes are often cheaper and easier to prepare for larger numbers.

RICOTTA PANCAKES WITH BLUEBERRIES & RASPBERRY-SWIRLED BUTTER {MAKES 8 PANCAKES}

Spoil yourself with this simple and delicious brekkie. If you have any leftover raspberry-swirled butter, it tastes great on toast, too.

RASPBERRY-SWIRLED BUTTER

100 g (3½ oz/¾ cup) frozen raspberries
2 tablespoons caster (superfine) sugar
120 g (4¼ oz) butter, softened
1 tablespoon icing (confectioners') sugar

RICOTTA PANCAKES

150 g (5½ oz/1 cup) plain (all-purpose) flour
1 teaspoon bicarbonate of soda
1 free-range egg
55 g (2 oz/¼ cup) caster (superfine) sugar
80 g (2¾ oz) ricotta cheese
250 ml (9 fl oz/1 cup) buttermilk, plus extra if necessary
canola spray oil, for cooking
150 g (5½ oz/1 punnet) blueberries, to serve

1. Combine the raspberries in a small saucepan with the caster sugar and 2 tablespoons of water. Heat gently to thaw the berries then increase the heat and simmer for 2–4 minutes, or until most of the liquid has evaporated and a syrup forms. Remove from the heat, pour the raspberries and their syrup into a bowl and refrigerate until cold.
2. Use hand-held electric beaters to beat the butter and icing sugar together until pale and creamy. Fold in the chilled raspberry mixture briefly so it swirls through the butter. Set aside.
3. Sift the flour and bicarbonate of soda together into a large bowl. Make a well in the flour.
4. In a separate bowl, whisk the egg, caster sugar and ricotta together until smooth. Whisk in the buttermilk to combine then pour this mixture into the well in the flour and whisk until a smooth batter is achieved. Mix in 2–3 more tablespoons of buttermilk if needed, to make it just pourable.
5. Heat a large heavy-based non-stick frying pan over a medium heat. Lightly grease the pan using the spray oil. Add one-third of a cup of batter at a time and cook for 1–2 minutes, or until golden brown on the underside. Turn the pancakes over and cook for another 30 seconds, or until just cooked through. Remove to a plate and repeat with the remaining batter.
6. Stack up the pancakes on serving plates. Top with raspberry-swirled butter and blueberries and serve.

MAPLE BACON, ASPARAGUS, SMASHED AVOCADO & FETA ON TOAST {SERVES 2}

The Canadians are on to something: crispy, smoky bacon combined with the syrupy sweetness of maple syrup makes for a cracking pair. I think asparagus tastes best when it's grilled, pan-fried or barbecued rather than steamed or boiled. Try to find pencil-thin asparagus, which is tender and cooks quickly.

- 2–4 rashers of bacon
- 1½ tablespoons maple syrup
- 1 avocado, halved, stone removed and flesh scooped out
- juice of ½ a lemon
- 50 g (1¾ oz/⅓ cup) crumbled feta cheese
- 2 slices of crusty bread
- 1 tablespoon extra virgin olive oil
- 1 tablespoon butter
- 6–8 (1 bunch) spears of asparagus, woody ends snapped off
- 2 teaspoons balsamic vinegar (optional)

1. Preheat the oven to 180°C (350°F/Gas 4).
2. Line a baking tray with baking paper. Arrange the bacon in a single layer on the tray then brush with the maple syrup. Transfer to the oven and bake for 12–16 minutes, or until lightly browned and crisp. Alternatively, you can fry the bacon in a large frying pan until crisp, remove from the pan then brush with the maple syrup.
3. While the bacon does its thing, use a fork to mush the avocado and lemon juice together. Mix in half the feta. Set aside for serving.
4. When the bacon is almost done, get a large non-stick frying pan nice and hot over a medium heat and put your bread down in the toaster. Add the olive oil, butter, asparagus and a pinch of salt to the frying pan and cook for 2–3 minutes, or until the asparagus is bright green but still retains some bite.
5. Put a piece of toast on each plate. Spoon half of the avocado mix over each one then top with the bacon and asparagus. Sprinkle over the remaining crumbled feta and drizzle over some balsamic vinegar (if using). Serve immediately.

PEAR & DRIED FIG BIRCHER MUESLI

{SERVES 2}

This recipe reminds me of eating far too many muesli samples in one sitting with my mates from the Thankyou™ team. Each box of muesli sold funds a week's food for a person in a developing country, so it was vital we got the flavours bang-on to help as many people as possible! Out of all the muesli we ate, pear and fig was one of our favourite combinations. It sounds like a pain having to mix it together the night before, but it makes a healthy and delicious breakfast in only seconds in the morning.

75 g (2¾ oz/¾ cup) rolled (porridge) oats
80 ml (2½ fl oz/⅓ cup) milk
80 ml (2½ fl oz/⅓ cup) apple or orange juice
¼ teaspoon ground cinnamon
4 dried figs, knobbly tips cut off, flesh roughly chopped or you can substitute figs for 50 g (1¾ oz/ ¼ cup) of sultanas (golden raisins)
1 green pear
130 g (4½ oz/½ cup) thick Greek yoghurt, to serve
3 tablespoons slivered almonds
1 tablespoon pepitas (pumpkin seeds), to serve
honey, to serve

1. The night before, combine the rolled oats, milk, juice, cinnamon and chopped figs in a medium bowl. Stir together, cover with plastic wrap then put in the refrigerator overnight.
2. In the morning, coarsely grate the pear then stir it into the muesli with the yoghurt and 1 tablespoon of the almonds.
3. Divide between two bowls. Scatter over the pepitas and remaining almonds then drizzle with honey.

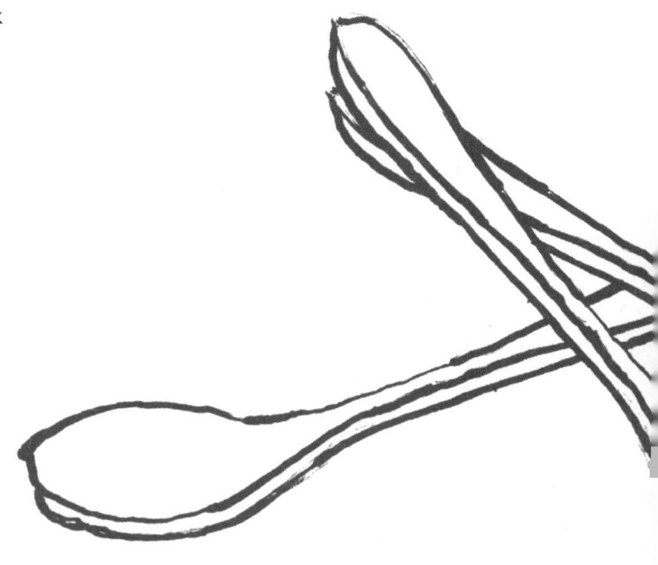

PAIN PERDU WITH HONEY VANILLA RICOTTA & SUMMER FRUIT {SERVES 2}

Pain perdu is essentially fancy French toast, and it's easy but impressive when you're making brekkie for friends. Good bakeries will have brioche; a bread made with eggs and butter to give it an almost cake-like crumb. Banana bread, raisin toast or panettone would work equally well.

1. Bring the milk to the boil in a small saucepan. Meanwhile, whisk the egg yolks, caster sugar and cinnamon together in a large bowl. Pour the boiling milk over the egg mixture, whisking constantly to combine.
2. Heat a non-stick frying pan over a medium–high heat and spray with oil, ensuring there is an even coating. Soak both sides of the sliced bread in the milk mixture. Transfer to the pan and cook for 1–2 minutes per side, or until golden brown. Fry on the four edges of each slice briefly then move to two serving plates.
3. Stir the vanilla bean paste and ricotta together in a small bowl. Spoon this mixture over the brioche. Top with sliced fruit, drizzle with honey and serve immediately.

170 ml (5½ fl oz/⅔ cup) milk
2 free-range egg yolks
1 tablespoon caster (superfine) sugar
½ teaspoon ground cinnamon
2 thick slices of day-old brioche or bread, crusts removed
canola spray oil, for cooking
1 teaspoon vanilla bean paste
115 g (4 oz/½ cup) low-fat ricotta cheese
sliced fruit, to serve, such as peaches, plums, berries or figs
1 tablespoon honey

SMOKED SALMON, ASPARAGUS & RICOTTA FRITTATAS {MAKES 12}

These muffin-sized frittatas are awesome for a weekend brekkie, but I also like to take them with me for a snack on the run. The eggs make it filling and the saltiness from the smoked salmon makes me want to keep eating them! When out of season, swap asparagus for frozen peas.

canola spray oil, for greasing
6–8 (1 bunch) spears of asparagus, woody ends snapped off, stems sliced into 2 cm (¾ inch) pieces, tips left whole
6 free-range eggs
60 ml (2 fl oz/¼ cup) milk
115 g (4 oz/½ cup) ricotta cheese
150 g (5½ oz) smoked salmon, torn into 2 cm (¾ inch) pieces
1 tablespoon finely chopped dill

1. Bring a medium saucepan of water to the boil over a medium–high heat. Preheat the oven to 190°C (375°F/Gas 5). Lightly grease a 12-hole (60 ml/2 fl oz/¼ cup) muffin tin with canola oil, then line each muffin hole with baking paper.
2. Add the sliced asparagus to the boiling water and blanch for 1–2 minutes, or until bright green and almost tender. Drain well.
3. Whisk together the eggs, milk, a pinch of salt and half of the ricotta. Stir through the drained asparagus, salmon and dill. Divide the mixture evenly between the muffin holes and crumble over the remaining ricotta.
4. Bake for 15–20 minutes, or until golden and puffy. Serve warm with a salad as a meal, or cold as a snack.

MUSHROOM, SPINACH & OLIVE TAPENADE BREAKFAST WRAP {SERVES 2}

Mushrooms love salty ingredients like feta, anchovies, bacon and certainly olives. Add a fried egg to each wrap or a grilled rasher of bacon if you want it to be a little more substantial.

1. Make your olive and dried fig tapenade.
2. Heat the largest frying pan you own over a medium–high heat with the canola oil. Add the mushrooms and fry, without moving them, for 1–2 minutes. Toss the mushrooms around and cook for a further 3–4 minutes, or until browned on all sides.
3. Season with salt, and add the butter and thyme leaves (if using). Once the butter has melted and foamed, toss everything in the pan around then remove the pan from the heat.
4. Generously spread about 2 tablespoons of the olive and dried fig tapenade around the middle of each warmed wrap or tortilla. Top each with the baby spinach and mushrooms, then spoon over the ricotta. Top with a little grated parmesan if you like. Fold up the bottom of the wrap to the middle, fold in the two sides and serve immediately.

1 batch of olive and dried fig tapenade (p. 173)
1 tablespoon canola oil
8 button mushrooms, quartered
1 tablespoon butter
4 thyme sprigs, leaves picked (optional)
2 large wraps or tortillas, warmed in a microwave or oven, to serve
2 large handfuls of baby English spinach
100 g (3½ oz) ricotta cheese, to serve
freshly grated parmesan cheese, to serve (optional)

CHILLI-SCRAMBLED EGG WITH RED ONION MARMALADE & ROAST CHERRY TOMATOES

{SERVES 2 HUNGRY PEOPLE OR 3 SLIGHTLY PECKISH FOLK}

ROAST CHERRY TOMATOES

250 g (9 oz/1 punnet) cherry tomatoes, halved
1 large garlic clove, sliced
2 tablespoons olive oil

CHILLI-SCRAMBLED EGGS

6 free-range eggs
80 ml (2½ fl oz/⅓ cup) milk
a few coriander (cilantro) or parsley sprigs, or chives, roughly chopped (optional)
2 tablespoons butter
1 long red chilli, seeded and thinly sliced (or ¼ teaspoon chilli flakes)

TO SERVE

a few slices of your favourite bread, toasted
red onion marmalade (p. 176) (or substitute with a store-bought chutney)

1. Crank your oven to 200°C (400°F/Gas 6).
2. Mix the cherry tomatoes in a bowl with the garlic, olive oil and a decent amount of salt and pepper. Transfer the tomatoes to a baking tray lined with baking paper, cut side facing up. Put the tomatoes in the oven and roast them for 20–30 minutes, or until they've shrivelled up a little and have darkened slightly. If in doubt, it's better to roast them for a longer rather than a shorter time; it creates the best flavour.
3. Make sure your bread is ready to be toasted, your red onion marmalade or chutney is on the table with a spoon in it, ready for dishing out, and your herbs (if using) are chopped and ready to go.
4. Heat a large heavy-based frying pan or saucepan over a medium heat. Crack the eggs into a bowl. If you get any shell in with the eggs, use half an eggshell to retrieve it and discard. Use a whisk or fork to beat the eggs, milk and chopped herbs together until combined.
5. Don't start this step until your tomatoes are almost done: add the butter and chilli or chilli flakes to the pan. Once the butter melts and foams, add the egg mixture. Let it sit for 20–30 seconds before slowly folding with a spatula or wooden spoon, making sure you get right to the bottom and edges of the pan. Toast the bread. When the eggs are about three-quarters done (there are still some runny bits), remove the pan from the heat. The residual heat will cook them through perfectly.
6. Spread the toast with the red onion marmalade, top with scrambled eggs and serve with the tomatoes.

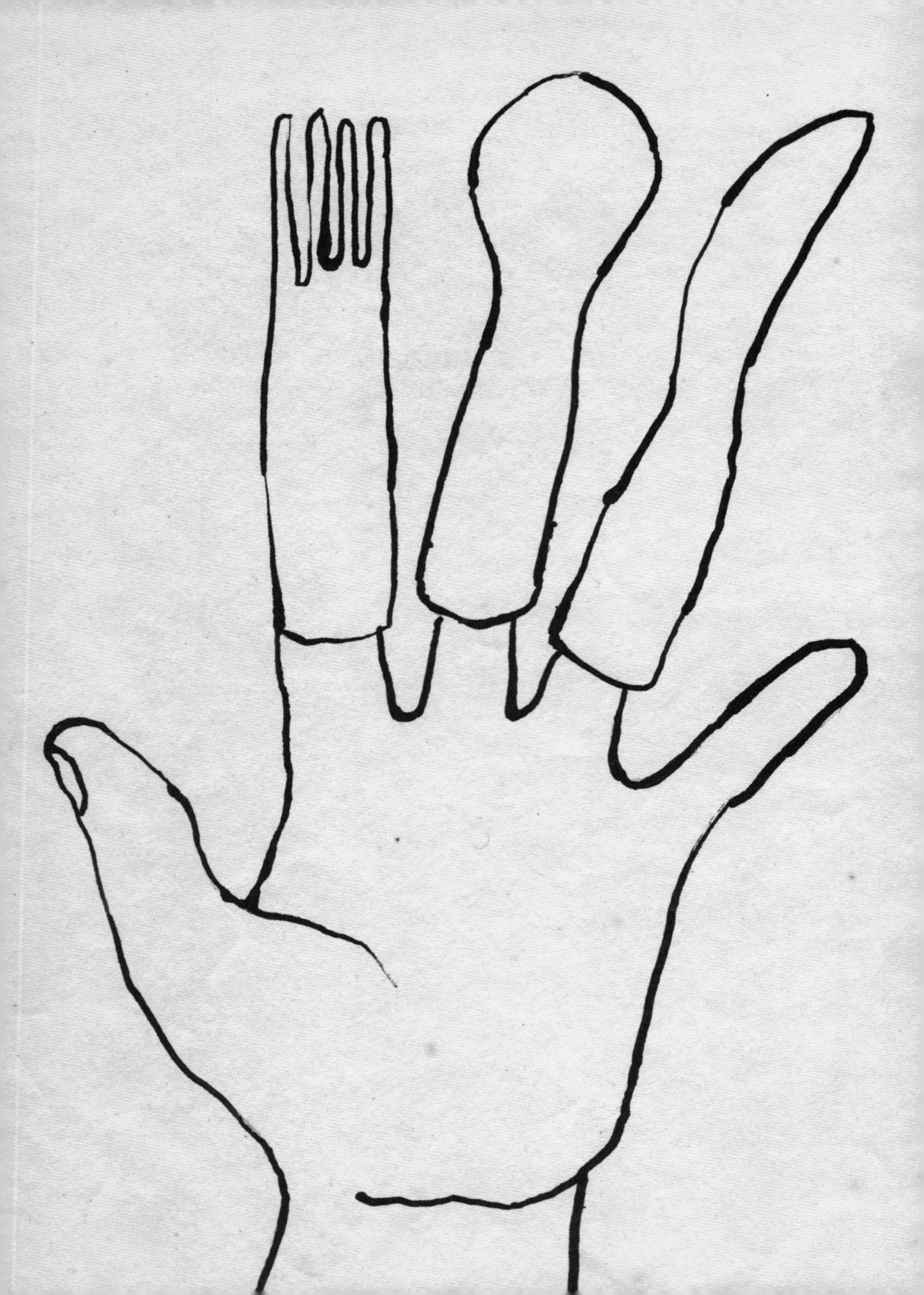

THINGS YOU CAN EAT WITH YOUR HANDS

I have (rather creatively) named this chapter 'Things you can eat with your hands' because it's full of things that you can ... errr ... eat with your hands. No cutlery required, although it's probably best not to wear your nicest white shirt when devouring these sorts of hand-held feasts! The dishes here are perfect if you're having mates around for a bite. Just make sure you get them to give you a hand with the washing-up afterwards!

PRAWN BANH MI {SERVES 4}

Banh mi takes all of the awesome things about Vietnamese flavours (that sweet, sour and salty goodness) and sticks it in a convenient roll. The pickle can be made well in advance, and the rest of the dish only takes minutes to put together. It's usually made with pork or duck, but I love how the prawns give you all those same flavours, but in a lighter, fresher way.

SANDWICHES

1½ tablespoons canola oil
16 raw prawns (shrimp), peeled and deveined
4 long soft white rolls, sliced open with a hinge like a book
1 Lebanese (short) cucumber, thinly sliced
a handful of torn mint or coriander (cilantro) leaves (or both!)
60 ml (2 fl oz/¼ cup) hoisin sauce (optional)
Kewpie mayonnaise (Japanese mayonnaise) or other good-quality mayo, to serve (optional)
chilli sauce (such as Sriracha), to serve (optional)

PICKLED CARROT & RADISH

125 ml (4 fl oz/½ cup) white vinegar
125 ml (4 fl oz/½ cup) water
55 g (2 oz/¼ cup) sugar
1 carrot, finely shredded
4 radishes, finely shredded or grated

1. Start this recipe at least 2 hours before you want to eat. To make the pickled carrot and radish, combine the vinegar, water and sugar in a saucepan. Cook over a medium heat until the sugar has completely dissolved then remove from the heat and leave to cool. Combine the carrot and radish in a glass or ceramic container, and pour over the cooled pickling liquid. Leave for 2–4 hours, or overnight if you can.
2. Heat a heavy-based frying pan over a high heat. Add the canola oil, then the prawns. Season with a pinch of salt and cook for 1 minute, tossing occasionally until golden and just cooked through. Move the prawns to a plate.
3. Drain the pickled carrot and radish. Stuff the rolls with cucumber, herbs, the carrot and radish pickle and the prawns. Add a few drizzles of the sauces if you like. Serve warm.

JERK-RUBBED BLACKENED CHICKEN SANDWICH WITH PINEAPPLE SALSA {SERVES 4}

The sugar in the jerk rub gives the chicken its blackened look, which translates into an awesome charred flavour that works perfectly with the sweet-and-sour pineapple salsa.

1. Combine the pineapple, cucumber, onion and coriander leaves in a bowl then set aside.
2. Mix all of the ingredients for the jerk rub together in a large bowl.
3. Cut each chicken thigh into five or six even pieces. Place these in the bowl with the jerk rub and mix around really well to coat. Heat the canola oil in a large heavy-based frying pan over a high heat. Add the chicken and cook for 2–3 minutes, then turn over and cook for a further 2–3 minutes, or until just cooked through (piping hot flesh with no sign of pink in the juices). Remove the chicken from the pan.
4. If you want your buns toasted, cut them in half and stick them under a hot grill (broiler), cut side up, to toast lightly for a minute or two.
5. Mix the lime juice through the pineapple salsa. Spread the toasted buns with a little Kewpie mayo (if using) then top with the chicken and pineapple salsa. Serve immediately.

¼ of a pineapple, skin and core removed, flesh cut into 5 mm (¼ inch) dice
1 Lebanese (short) cucumber, halved lengthways, seeded and cut into 5 mm (¼ inch) dice
½ a red onion, cut into 5 mm (¼ inch) dice
2 large handfuls of coriander (cilantro), leaves picked
4 boneless, skinless free-range chicken thighs
1½ tablespoons canola oil
4 large soft white buns
juice of 1 lime
Kewpie mayonnaise (Japanese mayonnaise) or other good-quality mayo, to serve (optional)

JERK RUB

1 teaspoon ground allspice
2 teaspoons ground coriander
1 teaspoon brown sugar
2 teaspoons onion powder
a pinch of chilli powder (about ⅛ teaspoon)
½ teaspoon salt, plus plenty of freshly ground black pepper

CRUNCHY BAKED CHICKPEAS

{MAKES 400 G (14 OZ)}

These chickpeas make a healthy snack instead of chips or popcorn when you're watching a movie. They are also great to take in a little container when you have to eat on the run.

1 x 400 g (14 oz) tin of chickpeas
½ teaspoon sea salt flakes
2 teaspoons smoked paprika
2 teaspoons ground cumin
2 teaspoons mild curry powder
¼ teaspoon chilli flakes (optional)

1. Preheat the oven to 150°C (300°F/Gas 2). Line a baking tray with baking paper. Drain and rinse the chickpeas really well, then drain again and transfer to a large bowl. Add all of the spices and mix around in the bowl to evenly coat the chickpeas.
2. Transfer the chickpeas to the lined tray, spreading them out in an even layer. Roast for 45–60 minutes, or until golden and crunchy. Allow to cool, then dig in.

PEA, TOMATO & FETA BRUSCHETTA

{SERVES 2}

This festive-coloured bruschetta is a treat when you have friends over, but it's just as good paired with poached eggs and crispy bacon for Sunday brunch.

1. Preheat the oven to 200°C (400°F/Gas 6). Arrange the sliced baguette on a baking tray then drizzle or brush over the olive oil. Bake in the oven for 10 minutes, or until lightly golden and crisp.
2. Blanch the peas, broad beans or soya beans for 2 minutes in salted boiling water, or until they are just tender. Drain, refresh with cold water and drain again. Transfer them to a mortar and pestle, add a pinch of salt and pound them up until there are some smooth bits and some chunky bits. Stir in the lemon zest and juice, a drizzle of extra virgin olive oil, the cherry tomatoes and feta.
3. Spoon this mixture over the baguette slices. Sprinkle over some parmesan or pecorino and serve immediately.

1 baguette, sliced 1 cm (½ inch) thick
olive oil, to taste
310 g (10½ oz) podded peas, broad beans or soya beans
zest and juice of 1 lemon
extra virgin olive oil
125 g (4½ oz/¾ cup) cherry tomatoes, halved or quartered
50 g (1¾ oz) feta cheese, crumbled (or substitute goat's cheese)
freshly grated parmesan or pecorino cheese, to serve

ZUCCHINI & HALOUMI FRITTERS

SERVES 2 (MAKES 4 LARGE FRITTERS)

Who says zucchini is boring? We've made these fritters in our Sprout kids class, and the students absolutely loved them. The haloumi makes these so moreish! Any leftover fritters refrigerate well, and make a great lunch to take to work the following day.

2 zucchini (courgettes)
80 g (2¾ oz/½ cup) grated haloumi cheese
3 spring onions (scallions), ends removed, thinly sliced on an angle
3 tablespoons chopped flat-leaf (Italian) parsley
1 free-range egg, lightly beaten
2 tablespoons plain (all-purpose) flour
2 tablespoons olive oil

1. Coarsely grate the zucchini onto a piece of paper towel then squeeze out any excess moisture. Add to a large bowl with all the other ingredients, except the olive oil, and mix together. Once everything has come together, use your clean hands to form four fritters slightly smaller than the palm of your hand. Place these on a lined baking tray or large plate then refrigerate for 15–30 minutes to help them firm up slightly.
2. Preheat a large non-stick frying pan over a high heat, add the olive oil and cook the fritters in batches. Fry until golden on both sides then serve immediately.

NUMBER 2 BURGER {SERVES 6}

One of my favourite places to eat in Adelaide is Burger Theory, owned by Dan Mendelson and Rob Dean. These guys have a cult following – some say they make the best burgers in the city, and I can't disagree. Without fail, I order the humbly named Number 2 Burger, which comes with pancetta, caramelised onions and blue cheese sauce. I know what you're thinking: blue cheese sauce?! But trust me, the cheese adds a delicious richness and saltiness to the dish, and it's not a strong blue cheese flavour, so it's well worth a try. Ask your butcher to mince some chuck steak for you; that's guaranteed to give you a tasty, juicy burger. Otherwise, any beef mince will do provided it's not lean or the burger will be dry.

BURGERS

800 g (1 lb 12 oz) minced (ground) chuck steak or other beef mince
2 tablespoons canola oil
6 rashers of bacon, halved, or 12 slices of prosciutto or pancetta
6 soft brioche-style burger buns, toasted under a grill (broiler) if you like
red onion marmalade, to serve (p. 176)

BLUE CHEESE SAUCE

50 g (1¾ oz) blue cheese, crumbled into small pieces
95 g (3¼ oz/⅓ cup) thick Greek yoghurt
85 g (3 oz/⅓ cup) sour cream

1. Combine all the ingredients for the blue cheese sauce in a small food processor or blender. Pulse a few times until the ingredients are just combined, don't over-blend or the sour cream might split. Alternatively, you can crumble the blue cheese as small as possible then whisk it into the yoghurt and sour cream. Refrigerate for at least 30 minutes to let the flavours develop. Any leftover sauce will keep in the fridge for a week.
2. Divide the beef mince into six equal portions and shape each one into a patty about 2 cm (¾ inch) thick. The diameter of the patty will shrink to about three-quarters of its original size after cooking, so make sure the patties are slightly larger than the buns you'll be serving them in.
3. Heat a large frying pan (or two medium frying pans) with 1 tablespoon of the canola oil over a high heat. Add the bacon and cook until crisp on both sides. Drain on some paper towel.
4. Add the remaining canola oil to the pan. Season both sides of each patty generously with salt then put in the pan and cook for 3–4 minutes, or until the burger develops a deep golden brown crust on the bottom. Turn the burgers over and reduce the heat to medium–high. Cook for another 3–4 minutes, or until the patties are just cooked. Remove from the pan to rest until serving.
5. Smear each bun base with red onion marmalade, then top with a patty, bacon, a little blue cheese sauce and a bun lid. Eat immediately, or I will.

CHIMICHURRI STEAK SANDWICH

{SERVES 4}

This is a monster of a sandwich that combines delicious charred juicy meat with a herby chimichurri sauce. Choose a nice thickly sliced loaf of bread that is crusty on the outside and soft in the middle.

STEAK SANDWICH

1 batch of chimichurri, to serve (p. 179)
2 tablespoons canola oil
2 thick porterhouse steaks (approx. 250–300 g/9–10½ oz)
wholegrain mustard (optional)
8 slices of sourdough or another crusty bread, or 4 baguettes
a handful of rocket (arugula), to serve
good-quality mayonnaise, to serve

1. Make the chimichurri.
2. Heat a large frying pan over a high heat. Add the canola oil. Season the steaks generously with salt and lots of freshly ground black pepper then put them in the pan. Cook for 3–4 minutes, or until they're a deep golden brown and a little charred on the bottom. Turn over and cook for a further 2–3 minutes, or until they are cooked to your liking.
3. Move the steaks to a chopping board and allow them to rest for 3 minutes before slicing into 5 mm (¼ inch) thick pieces. Spread some mustard over four pieces of bread if you like, then top with the slices of steak, a spoonful of chimichurri, some rocket, a squeeze of mayo and finish with another slice of bread. Serve the sandwiches immediately.

SPICY CHICKEN TACOS WITH APPLE & CABBAGE SALSA {SERVES 4}

These tacos make perfect party food. Get a big stack of small soft tortillas and chuck them in the middle of your table along with the spicy chicken and salsa. Use chicken thighs for these rather than boring ol' breast, to ensure they stay nice and juicy.

TACOS

1½ tablespoons vegetable oil
4 boneless, skinless free-range chicken thighs, sliced into thin strips
2 teaspoons ground cumin
2 teaspoons smoked paprika
1 red onion, halved and thinly sliced
8 small tortillas, to serve

APPLE & CABBAGE SALSA

1 granny smith apple, cored and julienned or coarsely grated
⅛ of a white cabbage, sliced as thinly as you can
3 radishes, sliced as thinly as you can (or use a mandolin)
2 tablespoons lime juice
2 tablespoons extra virgin olive oil
a handful of coriander (cilantro) leaves, torn

1. Make the salsa first by combining the apple, cabbage, radish, lime juice, extra virgin olive oil and a pinch of salt in a medium bowl. Add the coriander leaves right before serving.
2. Heat the vegetable oil in a large frying pan over a high heat. Toss the chicken in a bowl with the cumin, paprika and a pinch of salt then put in the pan and cook for 2 minutes on each side, or until browned and just cooked through (piping hot flesh with no sign of pink in the juices).
3. Move the chicken to a clean bowl and put the pan back on the stove. Lower the heat to medium then add the onion and cook until softened. Remove from the pan and add to the chicken. Gently combine.
4. Fill the tortillas with the chicken and onion mixture, top with a spoonful or two of salsa and serve.

SALTED CARAMEL POPCORN FUDGE

{MAKES 16 PIECES}

My birthday is the perfect time to request whatever the heck I want to eat. Every year, I ask Chloe to make me a batch of her signature fudge. It's completely over-the-top and decadent, and I love it. It has a rich, butterscotch taste that's cut by the salt flakes on the top, and the popcorn is the perfect foil to the fudge. I keep pestering her to open her own shop so I can have access to it more often. If you see her, please pester her for me.

125 g (4½ oz/½ cup) butter
330 g (11¾ oz/1½ cups, firmly packed) brown sugar
1 x 395 g (14 oz) tin of condensed milk
2 tablespoons golden syrup
180 g (6¼ oz) white chocolate melts
½ teaspoon sea salt flakes
enough air-popped salted popcorn to cover the surface of the tin (about 2 cups of popped corn)

1. Line a 21 cm (8¼ inch) square baking tin with baking paper. Melt the butter over a high heat in a medium heavy-based saucepan. Once melted, add the brown sugar, condensed milk and golden syrup. Stir until boiling then lower the heat to medium–low and cook for a further 10 minutes, stirring constantly. Keep an eye on it throughout; if it looks too hot, take it off the heat and keep stirring for a few seconds before returning it to the heat. Don't even think about touching or tasting it at this point, as caramel can burn pretty badly. The mixture will become thicker and darker in colour as it cooks.
2. Once ready (when the sugar has all dissolved and the mixture is smooth, dark and has thickened slightly), take the pan off the heat and add the chocolate. Vigorously stir in until smooth then pour into the lined tin using a spatula or wooden spoon to help spread it out evenly.
3. Working quickly, sprinkle the salt flakes all over the top, and scatter over the popcorn until the fudge is all covered. Lightly press the popcorn into the still-warm fudge. Place in the fridge to set for at least 1 hour.
4. Once set, take it out of the fridge and slice into 16 pieces. Some popcorn will fall off during this process, but that's fine. It's best served at room temperature so put it in an airtight container and keep in a cool corner of the kitchen for a few days. It might last longer, but I've never seen it survive more than a couple of days!

NO TIME TO COOK

I know cooking is probably the last thing on your mind sometimes. You're flat out, wishing that there were a way you could squeeze more than twenty-four hours into a day. But, unless you have a friend called Doc and drive a DeLorean, it's unlikely you'll be able to alter the space–time continuum, so you can only change your own actions. This is why it's super-handy to have a few really quick dishes in your repertoire rather than getting takeaway or petrol station snacks. Your wallet and taste buds will thank you for it.

CHORIZO, CHICKEN & CAPSICUM COUSCOUS

{SERVES 4 AS A LIGHT LUNCH OR 2 AS A SUBSTANTIAL DINNER}

How's that name for alliteration?! This dish is sort of like paella in that it has similar flavours and ingredients, but takes a fraction of the time to cook. Couscous is a great ingredient to have in your pantry because it cooks in about two minutes. I often make this dish with 200 g (7 oz) of peeled prawns (shrimp) instead of the chicken, and add them at the same time as the garlic and spices but, let's be honest, the P in prawn doesn't fit my alliterative recipe name nearly as well as chicken.

1½ tablespoons olive oil
1 chorizo sausage, thinly sliced
3 boneless, skinless free-range chicken thighs, cut into bite-sized pieces
1 small red capsicum (pepper), quartered, seeded and sliced into 5 mm (¼ inch) strips
3 garlic cloves, thinly sliced
2 teaspoons smoked paprika
2 teaspoons ground cumin
150 g (5½ oz/¾ cup) couscous
250 ml (9 fl oz/1 cup) good-quality chicken stock or water
2 handfuls of baby English spinach
juice of ½ a lemon
55 g (2 oz) kalamata olives, pitted
a handful of parsley or coriander (cilantro) leaves
thick Greek yoghurt, to serve

1. Heat a wide frying pan over a high heat. Add the olive oil, then the chorizo, chicken and capsicum. Cook, turning everything occasionally, for 5 minutes, or until the chicken is evenly browned.
2. Add the garlic, paprika and cumin, and stir to coat for 30 seconds or so. Add the couscous, stir, then pour in the chicken stock or water and stir again. Simmer for 1–2 minutes, or until the couscous has absorbed the liquid and is tender and the chicken is cooked through (piping hot flesh with no sign of pink in the juices).
3. Stir through the spinach, lemon juice and olives. As soon as the spinach has wilted, remove the pan from the heat, scatter over the parsley or coriander and serve with yoghurt.

TWO QUESADILLAS

Quesadillas (kay-sa-dee-ahs) were everywhere when I travelled around Mexico and the US. In fact, if I had a dollar for every quesadilla I ate, I'd have enough money to buy another quesadilla! They are basically fresh, flavoursome toasted sandwiches made with tortillas. If you have a flat toasty-toasty machine, you can make these in that rather than a frying pan. Serve the quesadillas with the Best. Guacamole. Ever. on page 174.

ZUCCHINI & PRAWN QUESADILLAS

{SERVES 2}

If you have a friend who doesn't like seafood, this dish is a great way to convince them how good it is. When you chop up prawns like you do here they cook incredibly quickly, so don't be tempted to walk away while they're in the pan or they'll become overcooked and rubbery.

1½ tablespoons canola oil
2 zucchini (courgettes), cut into 5 mm–1 cm (¼–½ inch) dice
1 large garlic clove, thinly sliced
16 raw prawns (shrimp), peeled, deveined and roughly chopped
4 large tortillas (or 8 small tortillas)
90 g (3¼ oz/⅔ cup, loosely packed) coarsely grated mozzarella cheese
45 g (1¾ oz/½ cup, loosely packed) coarsely grated parmesan cheese
2 tablespoons chopped jalapeños (available in jars in the Mexican section of most supermarkets)
a small handful of coriander (cilantro) leaves (optional)
1 lime, cut into wedges, to serve

1. Heat a medium non-stick frying pan over a high heat. Add the canola oil, then the diced zucchini. Fry for 1 minute, stirring once or twice, before adding the garlic and chopped prawns. Fry until the prawns are just cooked through (about 1–2 minutes). Transfer the zucchini mixture to a bowl and set aside.
2. Wipe out the pan with paper towel then put it back over the heat. Add a tortilla to the pan. Top with a quarter of the mozzarella and a quarter of the parmesan. Sprinkle over a quarter of the chopped jalapeños, then a quarter of the zucchini mixture and a few coriander leaves (if using).
3. When the tortilla is golden brown and the cheese has melted a little, carefully fold half of the tortilla onto itself, almost like an omelette.
4. Remove from the pan and repeat the process with the remaining tortillas and ingredients.
5. Cut each quesadilla into wedges and serve with wedges of lime.

MUSHROOM & CORN QUESADILLAS

{SERVES 2}

I grew up eating frozen corn, but I reckon it's worth the extra effort here to cut it from the cob yourself. If you're a bit of a carnivore, a sliced chorizo cooked with the mushrooms would be a tasty addition.

1. Heat a medium non-stick frying pan over a high heat. Add 1½ tablespoons of the canola oil, then the sliced mushrooms. Cook for 2–3 minutes on each side, or until golden brown and tender. Remove the mushrooms and set aside.
2. Add the remaining canola oil and the corn kernels to the pan. Cook for 1–2 minutes, or until lightly browned. Add a pinch of salt, the garlic, spring onions and cumin. Cook for a further minute before returning the mushrooms to the pan and adding the jalapeños. Stir to combine then transfer this mixture to a bowl.
3. Wipe out the pan with paper towel then put it back over the heat. Add a tortilla to the pan and top with a quarter of the mozzarella and parmesan. Spoon a quarter of the mushroom and corn mixture over the cheese. When the tortilla is golden brown and the cheese has melted a little, carefully fold half of the tortilla onto itself, almost like an omelette.
4. Remove from the pan and repeat the process with the remaining tortillas and ingredients.
5. Cut each quesadilla into wedges and serve with wedges of lime.

2 tablespoons canola oil
2 large mushrooms (such as portobello), thinly sliced
2 cobs of corn, kernels sliced off, core discarded
2 garlic cloves, thinly sliced
3 spring onions (scallions), thinly sliced
2 teaspoons ground cumin
2 tablespoons chopped jalapeños (available in jars in the Mexican section of your supermarket)
4 large tortillas (or 8 small tortillas)
90 g (3¼ oz/⅔ cup, loosely packed) coarsely grated mozzarella cheese
45 g (1¾ oz/½ cup, loosely packed) coarsely grated parmesan cheese
1 lime, cut into wedges, to serve

BEEF, BEAN & LYCHEE SALAD

{SERVES 2}

We've cooked this recipe at a couple of Sprout classes and found that it can be on the table in less than 20 minutes if we work smartly. An added bonus is that it's fresh and light, so it's great for summer or for those nights you feel like a lighter meal. Get the water on for the beans straight away and start cooking the beef while you prep the veg. If you're feeding another person or two, or if you're famished, you can serve the salad with steamed rice.

½ a batch of Vietnamese dressing (p. 115)
2 tablespoons shredded coconut
a large handful of green beans
1½ tablespoons canola oil
2 x 200 g (7 oz) of your favourite beef steaks
250 g (9 oz) cherry tomatoes
8 lychees, peeled and pitted (preferably fresh, but tinned are OK if fresh aren't available)
a large handful of bean sprouts
a large handful of mint leaves, roughly torn
2 tablespoons cashew nuts

1. Make the Vietnamese dressing.
2. Heat a medium frying pan (big enough to cook the steaks in later) over a high heat. Add the coconut to the dry pan and cook, stirring and tossing around constantly, until the coconut is lightly golden and fragrant. Transfer to a small bowl until ready to use.
3. Bring a big saucepan of salted water to the boil. Trim and discard the ends of the beans then cut the beans in half. Drop them into the boiling water with a pinch of salt and cook for 2 minutes. Drain the beans in a colander, then run them under cold water for 20 seconds or so, to stop them cooking any further. Drain again and put aside.
4. Wipe out the frying pan you used for the coconut then put it back over a high heat. Add the canola oil. Season the steaks with a few pinches of salt then add them to the pan. Cook for 3–4 minutes, or until golden brown and nicely seared on one side. Turn over and cook for a further 2–3 minutes, or until the steaks are cooked to your liking.
5. Halve the cherry tomatoes, quarter the lychees and combine them in a bowl with the beans, toasted coconut, bean sprouts, mint and cashews.
6. Remove the beef from the pan to a chopping board and rest for 2–3 minutes. Pour a small amount of the dressing over the steak as it rests. Add the dressing to the salad and toss gently to combine.
7. Slice the beef thickly and serve it with the salad. Make sure you drizzle over any remaining dressing from the chopping board!

THAI SALMON FISH CAKES WITH SHAVED CUCUMBER SALAD

{MAKES EIGHT 6 CM (2½ INCH) PATTIES/ENOUGH FOR 4 PEOPLE}

I love using salmon to make fish cakes as the fish is rich enough to handle a good bout of frying yet still remain juicy and delicious. I like to snack on these warm or cold, dipped in a little sweet-salty-and-sour sauce, or as served here, with a simple cucumber salad.

½ a batch of Vietnamese dressing (p. 115), to serve
400 g (14 oz) salmon fillets, skin off, flesh roughly chopped
2 teaspoons fish sauce (see note)
1 tablespoon red curry paste (see note)
1 free-range egg
30 g (1 oz/½ cup) panko breadcrumbs (see note)
3 spring onions (scallions), thinly sliced
cornflour (cornstarch), for dusting
2 tablespoons canola oil
2 Lebanese (short) cucumbers
2 red Asian shallots
a small handful of mint leaves
1 lime, cut into wedges, to serve

1. Make the Vietnamese dressing.
2. Combine the salmon, fish sauce, curry paste, a pinch of salt and the egg in a food processor. Mix until smooth then remove the bowl from the processor and stir in the breadcrumbs and spring onions by hand.
3. The mixture will be quite sticky so put a little cornflour on your hands to stop it from sticking to you. Form the mixture into eight patties about 1.5 cm (⅝ inch) thick. Dust the patties lightly with more cornflour.
4. Heat a medium heavy-based frying pan over a medium–high heat. Add the canola oil, then the salmon cakes in two batches. Cook for 2 minutes, or until golden brown, then carefully turn over with a spatula or egg slide and continue to fry until just cooked through. Remove from the pan to some paper towel and allow to cool slightly.
5. Use a vegetable peeler to shave thick ribbons of cucumber.
6. Peel and halve the shallots, then slice them as thinly as you can. Toss the cucumber, shallots and mint leaves with the Vietnamese dressing.
7. Serve the fish cakes with the cucumber salad and lime wedges for squeezing over.

Note: Fish sauce, red curry paste and panko breadcrumbs are all available in the Asian section of most supermarkets.

10-MINUTE WHITE BEAN & PARMESAN SOUP WITH BACON & PARSLEY BREADCRUMBS

{SERVES 1 HUNGRY PERSON OR 2 AS A LIGHTER MEAL}

Tinned beans are already cooked, which is why this soup is so quick to make. I have made this recipe to serve two for a light lunch or one for a more substantial dinner, but it can be easily multiplied if you are cooking for more. You will need a stick blender or bar blender for this recipe.

WHITE BEAN SOUP

2 tablespoons butter
2 garlic cloves, thinly sliced
1 x 400 g (14 oz) tin of cannellini beans, rinsed and drained
125 ml (4 fl oz/½ cup) milk
170 ml (5½ fl oz/⅔ cup) good-quality chicken or vegetable stock
2 tablespoons finely grated parmesan cheese
juice of ½ a lemon, to serve

BACON & PARSLEY BREADCRUMBS

2 tablespoons olive oil
2 rashers of bacon, rind removed, finely diced
1 long red chilli, seeded and thinly sliced
20 g (¾ oz/⅓ cup) breadcrumbs (I like panko breadcrumbs, see note on opposite page)
2 tablespoons shredded flat-leaf (Italian) parsley, plus extra to serve

1. Heat a medium saucepan over a medium heat. Add the butter and garlic and sweat for around 1–2 minutes, or until the butter is foaming and the garlic has softened. Add the cannellini beans, milk and stock, and cook, stirring occasionally, until the liquid comes to the boil. Boil for 30 seconds, add the parmesan, then remove the saucepan from the heat. Use a hand-held stick blender to purée the soup in the saucepan. Alternatively, you can transfer the contents of the saucepan to a bar blender and purée until smooth. Cover to keep warm, and put aside.
2. To make the bacon and parsley breadcrumbs, heat the olive oil in a large frying pan over a medium–high heat. Add the diced bacon and chilli, and cook, stirring often, until golden. Add the breadcrumbs and continue cooking, stirring often, until the breadcrumbs crisp up and turn slightly golden. Remove the pan from the heat and stir in the parsley.
3. Divide the soup between two bowls and stir a little lemon juice into each one. Spoon the bacon and parsley breadcrumbs over each serving. Sprinkle over a little extra shredded parsley and serve immediately.

CROQUE MONSIEUR (THE WORLD'S FANCIEST HAM & CHEESE TOASTIE)

{SERVES 2}

You can always rely on the French language to make the simplest of snacks sound like a super-fancy restaurant dish. This is essentially the toasted sandwich we all know and love, but with the addition of a thick, cheesy béchamel sauce to make it extra gooey and golden. You can swap the leg ham here with smoked salmon for an equally delicious and fancy toastie.

2 tablespoons butter, plus 2 more tablespoons, melted
1 tablespoon plain (all-purpose) flour
125 ml (4 fl oz/½ cup) milk
100 g (3½ oz/1⅓ cup, loosely packed) coarsely grated gruyere or cheddar cheese
4 thick slices of white bread
2–3 teaspoons dijon mustard, to taste
2 thick slices of good-quality leg ham

1. Heat a small saucepan over a medium heat. Add 2 tablespoons of butter and let it melt before adding the flour and whisking to combine. Cook for 30–60 seconds to cook the floury taste out, then whisk in the milk, a splash at a time. Simmer for 15–30 seconds, or until the béchamel mixture has thickened slightly. Whisk in half of the grated cheese until completely melted. If you love black pepper, add some now. Set aside to cool down a little.
2. Preheat your grill (broiler) to a medium–high heat. Brush one side of each slice of bread with the melted butter. Place onto a baking tray, buttered side up, then place under the grill for 1–2 minutes, or until golden.
3. Remove the bread to a plate or board, and spread the mustard evenly over the non-toasted side of two slices. Top with the ham and the remaining grated cheese. Place the topped slices of bread back on the tray then return to the grill and cook until the cheese melts and bubbles.
4. Remove the tray from the grill, top each base with a slice of bread, toasted side up. Spoon over the béchamel sauce and use the back of the spoon to smooth it into an even layer. Return to the grill one final time for 3–4 minutes, or until the béchamel is golden and bubbling.
5. Cut in half diagonally. Allow to cool briefly before hoofing in.

HONG PHAT
№198

BAKED MAC 'N' CHEESE WITH ROSEMARY BREADCRUMBS {SERVES 4}

Most mac and cheese recipes call for you to boil the pasta first, then combine it with a cheesy sauce before baking. But that means you have to boil, make a sauce and bake, right? This recipe uses a thinner-than-usual sauce, which means you can chuck it straight into the oven, saving time and washing-up. Heck yes!

MAC 'N' CHEESE

1½ tablespoons butter
1½ tablespoons plain (all-purpose) flour
330 ml (11¼ fl oz/1⅓ cups) milk
330 ml (11¼ fl oz/1⅓ cups) water
½ teaspoon salt
200 g (7 oz/2 cups) dried elbow macaroni
150 g (5½ oz/1½ cups, loosely packed) coarsely grated tasty cheddar cheese

ROSEMARY BREADCRUMBS

1 tablespoon olive oil
1½ tablespoons butter
2 short rosemary sprigs, leaves very finely chopped
2 garlic cloves, finely chopped
45 g (1½ oz/¾ cup) panko breadcrumbs (from the Asian section of most supermarkets)

1. Preheat the oven to 200°C (400°F/Gas 6) (fan-forced). Melt the butter in a medium saucepan over a medium–high heat then add the flour and continue to cook for a few minutes. Whisk for a minute to cook the floury flavour out, then whisk in the milk and water, a little at a time, to ensure a nice smooth sauce. Add the salt. Bring to the boil, then reduce to a simmer and cook for 5–10 minutes, or until the sauce thickens slightly.
2. Combine the macaroni and 100 g (3½ oz/1 cup) of the grated cheese in a small baking dish, about 18 × 23 cm (7 × 9 inches). Pour over the sauce. Try and make sure the macaroni is completely covered in the sauce, to ensure it cooks through evenly. Cover with foil then bake for 20–25 minutes, or until the pasta is just cooked.
3. Meanwhile, make the rosemary breadcrumbs. Heat the olive oil and butter together in a large frying pan over a medium heat. Add the rosemary and garlic. As soon as it smells delicious (about 10–20 seconds) add the breadcrumbs and a pinch of salt. Stir to combine. Remove from the heat and set aside until the macaroni is ready.
4. Remove the baking dish from the oven, discard the foil, scatter over the remaining cheese then the rosemary breadcrumbs. Return to the oven and bake until the top is golden brown (about 5–10 minutes). Remove from the oven, allow to cool slightly, then serve.

MICROWAVED CHOCOLATE & PEANUT BUTTER MUG PUDDING

{SERVES 1}

You know those nights when you really feel like a pudding for dessert but can't be bothered waiting for the oven to heat up? Here's your solution. Just a heads-up, this is a super-rich dessert, and I'm a big sweet tooth! Don't say I didn't warn you ...

1 free-range egg
2 tablespoons crunchy peanut butter
1 tablespoon icing (confectioners') sugar
2 teaspoons plain (all-purpose) flour
1 tablespoon unsweetened cocoa powder
30 g (1 oz/¼ cup) dark chocolate chips or chopped chocolate
a scoop of vanilla ice cream, to serve (optional)

1. Crack the egg into a small bowl and add the peanut butter, icing sugar, flour and cocoa powder. Whisk until the mixture is smooth and there are no big clumps of peanut butter left.
2. Stir through the chocolate chips then pour the batter into a 250 ml (9 fl oz/1 cup) capacity microwave-safe coffee mug or ramekin. Microwave on full power for 30 seconds. Don't cook it any longer than this or the egg will overcook and you'll be left with a chocolate omelette!
3. Give it a minute to cool down then eat it straight out of the mug with a scoop of vanilla ice cream, if you like.

TWO INSTANT FROZEN DESSERTS

Most frozen dessert recipes require either the services of an ice-cream machine or several hours in your freezer. Those recipes could never make it into this chapter! If you have a food processor or stick blender you are no more than five minutes away from a perfectly smooth sorbet or ice cream that's tastier than any supermarket or late-night convenience store frozen treat.

5-MINUTE MANGO & COCONUT ICE CREAM {SERVES 2}

This ice cream is perfect for a hot day. If mangoes are cheap, buy them, cut off the cheeks, scoop out the flesh and freeze it. Otherwise, many supermarkets sell frozen mango cheeks in a bag.

2 frozen mango cheeks, flesh scooped out (see above) and cut into 2 cm (¾ inch) chunks
60 ml (2 fl oz/¼ cup) coconut milk
2 good-quality waffle ice-cream cones, to serve (optional)
a small handful of blueberries, to serve

1. Combine the frozen mango and coconut milk in a small food processor and blend until smooth.
2. Scoop into pretty glasses, or into waffle cones (if using). Top with some blueberries. Serve immediately.

INSTANT RASPBERRY & CRANBERRY SORBET {SERVES 2}

It's crazy that such a great dessert can be made so quickly and with so few ingredients. Almost any frozen fruit will work, but I seem to always have a bag of raspberries lying around in the freezer. This recipe also makes a great slushie cocktail if you add a splash of vodka or gin.

120 g (4¼ oz/1 slightly heaped cup) frozen raspberries (pitted frozen cherries are a great alternative)
60 ml (2 fl oz/¼ cup) cranberry juice
6 mint leaves (optional)
2 good-quality waffle ice-cream cones, to serve (optional)

1. Combine the frozen raspberries, cranberry juice and mint leaves (if using) in a small food processor and blend until smooth.
2. Serve immediately, either in pretty glasses or waffle cones (if using).

WEEKNIGHT DINNERS

This chapter is possibly going to be the most useful to you on a standard day. Fancy cooking has a time and a place, but if you get home at 6:30 on a Wednesday night and just want a nice meal to end your day, these are the recipes for you. They are quick, easy to make and healthy. The recipes in this chapter also make brilliant leftovers; make a full batch of the recipe even if you're only cooking for one or two, then divide any remaining food into containers and, hey presto, tomorrow's lunch is ready to go.

CHICKEN & PEA KORMA WITH TZATZIKI {SERVES 4}

Korma is one of those please-all Indian curries. Everyone (except vegetarians), will pounce on a big bowl of this chicken one, and even then you could swap the chicken out for sweet potato or pumpkin (winter squash). Prepare for your kitchen to smell delicious. The green apple I've added to the tzatziki gives it a little extra zing.

- 130 g (4½ oz/½ cup) thick Greek yoghurt
- 3 garlic cloves, thinly sliced
- a thumb-sized piece of fresh ginger, finely grated
- a handful of coriander (cilantro), stems finely chopped, leaves reserved
- 1 tablespoon garam masala
- 6 boneless, skinless free-range chicken thighs
- cooked white rice or naan bread, to serve (optional)
- 2 tablespoons canola oil
- 1 brown onion, halved and thinly sliced
- ½ a red capsicum (pepper), seeded and thinly sliced
- 1½ tablespoons tomato paste (concentrated purée)
- 2 teaspoons curry powder
- ¼ teaspoon salt
- 1 batch of simple but proper tzatziki (p. 177. Leave out the dill.)
- 1 green apple (such as granny smith), coarsely grated, seeds removed
- 75 g (2½ oz/½ cup) frozen peas
- 25 g (1 oz/¼ cup) flaked almonds (optional)

1. In a large bowl, stir together the yoghurt, garlic, ginger, coriander stems and 2 teaspoons of the garam masala.
2. Cut each chicken thigh into nine pieces then stir into the yoghurt mixture, cover with plastic wrap and marinate in the fridge for at least 30 minutes, or ideally for 1–3 hours, if you have time.
3. If you are making rice, start it just before you start cooking the korma.
4. Heat a large heavy-based saucepan over a high heat. Add the canola oil, then the onion and capsicum and stir for 3–5 minutes, or until the onion starts to turn golden brown. Add the tomato paste, curry powder, salt and the remaining garam masala, and cook for a further 2–3 minutes, stirring frequently, before adding the chicken and yoghurt mixture.
5. Cook for 8–13 minutes, stirring often, or until the yoghurt has started to brown and the chicken has just cooked through (piping hot flesh with no sign of pink in the juices). Turn the heat off.
6. Meanwhile, make the tzatziki (omitting the dill in the recipe). Roughly chop half the coriander leaves and stir them through the tzatziki with the grated apple.
7. Stir the frozen peas through the korma. The second they have warmed through in the korma, put the taztziki in the middle of the table with the rice or naan bread.
8. Scatter over the remaining coriander leaves and flaked almonds (if using) and serve.

RICOTTA 'GNOCCHI' WITH BASIL, OLIVE & TOMATO SAUCE {SERVES 4}

To call this dish gnocchi is really a lie, but it is such a quick and tasty lie that it deserves a recipe anyway. Gnocchi are usually soft little potato dumplings, often served with a ragu, pesto or tomato sauce. Making the gnocchi with ricotta instead saves on all that potato cooking time, meaning you can have homemade gnocchi and sauce on the table before you can say 'Liar, liar pants on fire.' OK, well that last bit was a lie ... I made this recipe with a group of children aged between six and nine years old in a Sprout class and they nailed it. So yes, the pressure is on now, but that shows how simple it is!

1 batch of tomato and fennel multipurpose sauce (p. 178)
400 g (14 oz) ricotta cheese
2 free-range eggs
50 g (1¾ oz) parmesan cheese, coarsely grated, plus extra to serve
2 tablespoons plain (all-purpose) flour, plus extra for dusting
½ teaspoon freshly grated nutmeg
8 kalamata olives, pitted and quartered (optional)
a small handful of basil leaves, torn, smaller leaves left whole, to serve
canola spray oil

1. Make the tomato and fennel sauce then remove the pan from the heat but leave the sauce in the pan and cover it with a lid to keep warm.
2. Combine the ricotta, eggs, parmesan, flour, nutmeg and a good pinch of salt in a medium bowl and use a spatula or wooden spoon to beat everything together. Flour your hands, then roll tablespoons of the mixture into balls on a clean, floured work bench. Roll the balls in a little extra flour, then cook these 'gnocchi' in a saucepan of salted boiling water for 3–4 minutes, or until the dumplings firm up and float to the surface. Carefully remove the gnocchi with a slotted spoon.
3. Transfer the tomato sauce to a bowl and stir through the olives (if using) and most of the basil leaves.
4. Clean your pan, then get it back over a high heat with some spray oil. Add the boiled gnocchi carefully to the pan, and cook for 1–2 minutes, turning once, until golden.
5. Serve the ricotta gnocchi on top of the tomato sauce, scatter over some extra parmesan cheese, and the remaining basil leaves.

CAJUN FISH WITH SWEETCORN, RED ONION & SMOKED ALMOND SALAD

{SERVES 2}

Cajun flavours work really well with fish. Try and get fillets of fish that have their skin on for this recipe; the butter added at the end makes the skin golden and crunchy, like a fish version of pork crackling! Watch out for how much cayenne pepper you use because it's very hot if you go overboard. Check out my tips for pan-frying fish on page 21 before you get started.

1 batch of sweetcorn, red onion and smoked almond salad (p. 120)
4 thyme sprigs, leaves picked
1 teaspoon smoked paprika
a pinch of cayenne pepper
1 teaspoon ground cumin
1½ tablespoons canola oil
2 x 150–200 g (5½–7 oz) firm-fleshed white fish fillets, such as snapper or barramundi
1 tablespoon butter
2 lemon wedges, to serve

1. Get your sweetcorn, red onion and smoked almond salad under control.
2. Mix the thyme leaves, paprika, cayenne pepper, cumin and a good pinch of salt and freshly ground black pepper together in a small bowl. Rub this mixture all over the flesh side of both pieces of fish, avoiding the skin side.
3. Heat a large non-stick frying pan over a medium–high heat. Pour in the canola oil then add the fish, skin side down. Hold the fish down gently with a spatula or your hand for 10–15 seconds to ensure the skin stays flat against the pan and gets nice and crispy. Cook for 3–4 minutes, turn the fish over and add the butter. Cook for a further 2–3 minutes, basting the fish with the melted butter, until it's almost cooked through.
4. Put a piece of fish on each plate and serve immediately with a lemon wedge and the sweetcorn, red onion and smoked almond salad.

MINI PORK, FENNEL & ALLSPICE MEATBALLS WITH LONG PASTA

{SERVES 4}

It's really tempting when you are making meatballs to roll them into boulders, but it's worth taking the time to roll tiny little balls so everyone gets a little hoard of meatballs in their bowl. The small size also means they cook quickly and don't dry out. These meatballs would also be great served on the parmesan polenta on the opposite page.

1 tablespoon fennel seeds
500 g (1 lb 2 oz) minced (ground) pork
1 tablespoon dried oregano
1 tablespoon allspice
¼ teaspoon chilli flakes (optional)
½ teaspoon salt
¼ teaspoon freshly ground black pepper
1 batch of tomato and fennel multipurpose sauce (p. 178)
1½ tablespoons canola oil
250 g (9 oz) dried fettuccine, pappardelle or tagliatelle
a large handful of basil leaves, to serve
finely grated parmesan cheese, to serve

1. Heat a large frying pan over a high heat. Toast the fennel seeds for 1–2 minutes, or until fragrant. Tip into a large bowl and cool for a few minutes.
2. Add the pork mince to the fennel seeds along with the oregano, allspice, chilli flakes (if using), salt and pepper. Combine all the ingredients really well. Shape the pork into 2 cm (¾ inch) diameter meatballs and put them onto a plate. Cover with plastic wrap and refrigerate until you have your tomato sauce ready.
3. Make the tomato and fennel sauce, then remove the pan from the heat but leave the sauce in the pan and cover it with a lid to keep warm. Fill and boil the kettle.
4. Add the canola oil to the largest frying pan you own and place over a high heat. Add the meatballs and cook, turning occasionally, for about 2 minutes or until they are brown all over. Transfer the meatballs to the saucepan of sauce. Bring the sauce to a very gentle simmer, then immediately turn off the heat and cover with the lid. The residual heat will cook the meatballs through perfectly.
5. Meanwhile, pour the boiling water from the kettle into a large pot over a high heat. Cook the pasta according to the packet directions, or until *al dente* (cooked but still a little firm to the bite), then drain.
6. Serve the pasta immediately with the meatballs, sauce, basil leaves and some grated parmesan.

PAN-FRIED MUSHROOMS WITH PESTO & PARM POLENTA {SERVES 2}

Look for instant polenta for this dish as it cooks in minutes and saves a heck of a lot of stirring. Make sure you add the polenta slowly to the stock or water while whisking. If you just tip it in all at once, you're likely to get lumpy polenta. I like to let my polenta cool then slice and fry it because you get a delicious crisp crust and soft inside that is killer with the mushrooms.

- ½ a batch of simple balsamic dressing (p. 115)
- 1 batch of traditional pesto, to serve (p. 175)
- 2 cups (500 ml/17 fl oz) good-quality chicken stock or water
- 90 g (3¼ oz/½ cup) instant polenta
- 4 tablespoons butter
- 25 g (1 oz/¼ cup) finely grated parmesan cheese
- 90 ml (3 fl oz) canola oil
- 8 large mushrooms, such as field or portobello, sliced 5 mm (¼ inch) thick
- 5 thyme sprigs, leaves picked
- 2 garlic cloves, thinly sliced
- 40 g (1½ oz/¼ cup) hazelnuts, halved
- 2 large handfuls of rocket (arugula)

1. Make the dressing and pesto, then put aside.
2. Bring the chicken stock or water to the boil in a medium saucepan over a high heat. Slowly whisk in the polenta until it is all combined then turn the heat down to medium and cook, stirring constantly, until thickened (about 2–3 minutes).
3. Line a 12 × 20 cm (4½ × 8 inch) rectangular container (such as a lunchbox or biscuit tin) with baking paper. Remove the polenta from the heat, whisk in half of the butter and all of the parmesan. Taste to check the seasoning then pour into the container. Smooth out the top, and refrigerate for 25–30 minutes, or until set firmly.
4. Heat a large frying pan over a medium–high heat with 1½ tablespoons of the canola oil. Add half the mushrooms and a pinch of salt and fry until golden on both sides. Remove the mushrooms from the pan and repeat with another 1½ tablespoons of canola oil and the rest of the mushrooms.
5. Turn out the set polenta onto a chopping board. Cut into two 10 × 12 cm (4 × 4½ inch) rectangles. Wipe out the pan you used for the mushrooms, put it back over a high heat and add the remaining oil. Cook for 2–3 minutes on each side, or until golden and warmed through. Transfer to two serving plates.
6. Return all of the mushrooms to the hot pan. Season then scatter over the thyme leaves. Add the remaining butter, the garlic and hazelnuts. Toss and cook until the mushrooms are golden and tender.
7. Drizzle the dressing over the rocket and toss gently. Top each polenta slice with a few spoonfuls of pesto, the mushrooms and some rocket and serve.

GREEK LAMB WITH ROASTED CAPSICUM HUMMUS & CHARRED EGGPLANT

{SERVES 4}

Marinating the lamb in this way is something my dad used to do every time he cooked on the barbecue. He'd pick a lemon from the tree, yank a bit of rosemary from a potted plant, and 'source' the garlic (AKA buy some from the shops!). For the romantic notion of this recipe, let's pretend he grew the garlic himself, too.

- 2 lemons
- 2 rosemary sprigs, leaves picked
- 2 garlic cloves, crushed
- 2 tablespoons olive oil
- 8 lamb cutlets or loin chops
- 1 batch of roasted capsicum hummus (p. 176)
- 1 Lebanese (short) cucumber
- 1 tablespoon extra virgin olive oil,
- a handful of mint leaves
- a few dill sprigs
- 1 small eggplant (aubergine), sliced as thinly as you can
- a small handful of kalamata olives, pitted and quartered
- 95 g (3¼ oz/⅓ cup) thick Greek yoghurt, to serve

1. Cut 1 of the lemons in half and squeeze all of its juice into a large snap-lock bag. Add the rosemary leaves to the bag along with the garlic, olive oil and lamb cutlets. Seal the bag, give it a good shake around, and put it in the fridge to marinate for between 30 minutes and 4 hours.
2. Make the roasted capsicum hummus.
3. When the meat has finished marinating, heat a large non-stick frying pan over a high heat. Remove the lamb from the marinade, shaking off any excess, then add the cutlets to the pan. Cook for 2–3 minutes per side, or until the cutlets are cooked to your liking.
4. While the lamb cooks, use a vegetable peeler to quickly peel the cucumber into thin strips. Combine the cucumber in a bowl with the extra virgin olive oil, freshly squeezed juice of half a lemon, a pinch of salt and the mint and dill.
5. Remove the lamb to a chopping board to rest for a couple of minutes. Put the eggplant into the hot frying pan and cook over a medium heat for 1 minute on each side, or until cooked and a little charred.
6. Smear the roasted capsicum hummus over a big serving platter. Top with the eggplant, then the lamb. Drape the cucumber, mint and dill on top of the lamb, then scatter over the olives and serve immediately with some yoghurt on the side.

TWO GREAT MEXICAN CHILLIES

A great chilli is comfort food at its best. Don't let the name put you off – for me, there should be a little heat, but it shouldn't blow your head off. For chipotle chillies in adobo sauce, which are used for both chillies, have a look in specialty food stores, or online – in Australia you can try chilemojo.com.au. These recipes taste great when you make them, but they're even better the next day once the flavours have had a bit longer to mingle.

KIDNEY BEAN CHILLI WITH CORNBREAD {SERVES 4}

I've never been hugely into making bread – I get really impatient waiting for yeasty doughs to prove. Cornbread is different though; it has a great bready texture to soak up the chilli sauce, but it's no harder to make than any mix 'n' bake muffin. If you want to make this meal even more special, serve it with a batch of quick pickled cucumber and the Best.Guacamole.Ever. (pages 177 and 174).

KIDNEY BEAN CHILLI

2 tablespoons olive oil
1 brown onion, finely diced
3 garlic cloves, sliced
1 long red chilli, seeded and sliced
1 red capsicum (pepper), seeded and roughly diced
1 tablespoon ground cumin
1 tablespoon ground coriander
2 teaspoons smoked paprika
2 x 400 g (14 oz) tins of chopped tomatoes
2 chipotle chillies in adobo sauce, finely chopped (optional)
1 x 400 g (14 oz) tin of kidney beans, rinsed and drained
a handful of coriander (cilantro) leaves

CORNBREAD (MAKES 10)

canola spray oil, for greasing
230 g (about 8¼ oz/1¼ cups) polenta
110 g (3¾ oz/¾ cup) plain (all-purpose) flour
55 g (2 oz/¼ cup) caster (superfine) sugar
2 teaspoons salt
1 teaspoon baking powder
250 ml (9 fl oz/1 cup) milk
2 free-range eggs
2 tablespoons melted butter or olive oil

1. Preheat the oven to 220°C (425°F/Gas 7). Use canola spray oil to grease 10 holes of a 12-hole (60 ml/2 fl oz/¼ cup) muffin tin.
2. Combine all the dry ingredients for the cornbread in one bowl. Put the milk, eggs and butter (or olive oil) in another bowl and whisk until combined. Make a well in the centre of the dry ingredients and gradually pour in the milk mixture, whisking as you go, until it's smooth. Pour this batter into the greased muffin holes then transfer to the oven. Cook for 8–10 minutes, or until a skewer inserted in the centre of a muffin comes out clean. Turn out onto a wire rack and leave to cool.
3. Heat a large heavy-based saucepan over a medium heat with the olive oil. Fry the onion for 3–5 minutes, stirring occasionally, until lightly browned. Add the garlic, chilli, capsicum, spices and a pinch or two of salt, to taste. Cook for 2 more minutes, stirring, until everything looks fairly dry. Add the tomatoes and chipotle (if using). Cook for 10 minutes, or until all of the excess liquid has evaporated and the sauce has reduced down.
4. Add the kidney beans to the chilli, stir to combine and remove the pan from the heat. Cover and keep warm until ready to serve then roughly chop the coriander leaves, scatter them on top and serve with the cornbread, some pickled cucumbers and some guacamole (if you like).

KYLE'S CHILLI CON CARNE

{SERVES 4, WITH LEFTOVERS}

This Tex-Mex recipe is a cracker from my mate Kyle. He made an enormous cauldron-like pot of this chilli con carne to feed eighty people from what he could find in a hostel kitchen while on holiday. Although if you ask him, he might just tell you he cooked it for 150 people! His dream is to start a five-buck food truck. I can't wait to swing past and grab a big bowl of this chilli!

2 tablespoons olive oil
2 brown onions, finely diced
2 garlic cloves, sliced
1 capsicum (pepper), seeded and diced (whichever colour floats your boat)
1 tablespoon chilli sauce (such as Sriracha)
1 teaspoon smoked paprika
½ teaspoon chilli powder (add more if you love the burn!)
1 heaped teaspoon curry powder
1 kg (2 lb 4 oz) minced (ground) beef
1 x 400 g (14 oz) tin of chopped tomatoes
1 x 700 ml (24 fl oz) bottle of tomato passata (puréed tomatoes)
2 handfuls of coriander (cilantro) leaves (optional)
cooked white rice or a large bag of corn chips, to serve
250 g (9 oz) sour cream or thick Greek yoghurt
125 g (4½ oz/1¼ cups, loosely packed) coarsely grated cheddar cheese

1. Heat a large heavy-based frying pan over a medium–high heat. Chuck in the olive oil, onion, garlic and capsicum. Cook, stirring frequently, until the onion is translucent. Add the chilli sauce, paprika, chilli powder, curry powder and a good pinch of salt and freshly ground black pepper. Cook until fragrant and everything is golden.
2. Throw in your mince and brown it for a few minutes, stirring and jabbing at it frequently with a big wooden spoon to break it up.
3. Pour in the tomatoes and passata, bring to the boil, then reduce the heat and simmer for about 20–30 minutes, or until the sauce reduces, thickens and darkens slightly.
4. Throw in another nice pinch of salt and pepper and taste to assess the spice level. Sprinkle the chilli with coriander leaves (if using) and serve with some rice or a big handful of corn chips, a nice big dollop of sour cream or Greek yoghurt and a handful of grated cheese.

CLASSIC PAD THAI

{SERVES 2 AS A GENEROUS MAIN OR 4–6 AS PART OF A BANQUET}

Growing up, I never really liked pad Thai as it always seemed to be just a generic bland noodle dish ordered to bulk up takeaway meals. But I was lucky enough to taste a few freshly made versions on a recent holiday to Thailand and fell in love with it. Apparently, it was invented in the 1930s in a nationwide competition to devise a new noodle dish. I think maybe Australia should have a competition to figure out our national dish! To make this dish vegetarian, simply swap the fish sauce in the tamarind dressing for soy sauce.

- 1 batch of tamarind dressing (p. 115)
- 100 g (3½ oz) flat rice noodles (sometimes called pad Thai noodles)
- 2 tablespoons vegetable oil, plus extra for drizzling
- 3 red Asian shallots, thinly sliced
- 3 free-range eggs
- 95 g (3¼ oz/½ cup) diced, firm tofu
- 3 tablespoons chopped peanuts, plus extra for serving
- a large handful of bean sprouts, trimmed
- a handful of Chinese garlic chives, cut into 2.5 cm (1 inch) lengths or thinly sliced spring onions (scallions)
- a handful of coriander (cilantro) leaves, to serve (optional)
- lime wedges, to serve
- chilli sauce, such as Sriracha, to serve (optional)

1. Make your tamarind dressing.
2. Bring a big pot of water to the boil. Plunge the noodles into the water and boil for 2–4 minutes, or until just tender. Drain and toss in a drizzle of vegetable oil to keep them from sticking together.
3. Heat a wok over a high heat with the vegetable oil. Fry the shallots until lightly golden, then crack in the eggs and quickly mix them around until almost cooked.
4. Add the diced tofu and peanuts and move around for 30 seconds or so. Add the noodles then the tamarind dressing, and use tongs to toss and move the pad Thai around until all the liquid has been absorbed. Add most of the bean sprouts and the garlic chives or spring onions, mix together quickly, and remove the wok from the heat.
5. Scatter over the remaining bean sprouts and peanuts and the coriander leaves (if using). Serve with a few lime wedges, for squeezing over, and the chilli sauce on the table (if using).

COCOA-RUBBED CHICKEN DRUMSTICKS

{SERVES 4}

Drumsticks are one of the best value cuts of meat you'll find, which makes this a great dish for feeding a few friends. This South American style of flavouring drumsticks is great when they're served with the sweetcorn, red onion and smoked almond salad on page 120, or with the mixed tomato, caper, shallot, basil and mozzarella salad on page 116. These are also great just piled into a big bowl with some lime wedges so you can sit on the couch and munch into them with your mates. I suggest you have a couple of napkins or paper towels handy!

- 2 teaspoons unsweetened cocoa powder
- 1 teaspoon mustard powder
- ¼ teaspoon chilli powder
- 2 teaspoons smoked paprika
- 2 teaspoons ground cumin
- ¼ teaspoon salt
- ¼ teaspoon freshly ground black pepper
- 8 free-range chicken drumsticks
- 2 tablespoons canola oil
- 2 limes, cut into wedges

1. Preheat the oven to 190°C (375°F/Gas 5).
2. Line a big baking tray or roasting tin with baking paper. Combine the cocoa, mustard and chilli powders with the paprika, cumin, salt and black pepper in a large bowl. Toss the drumsticks, one at a time, in this spice mix until lightly coated.
3. Heat a large heavy-based frying pan over a high heat. Add half of the canola oil and half the drumsticks to the pan and cook, turning every 30 seconds, or until the drumsticks are brown all over. Remove the browned chicken and repeat with the remaining oil and drumsticks.
4. Once all of the drumsticks are browned and smell delicious, place them onto the baking tray or roasting tin and put them in the oven to bake for 25–30 minutes. Remove from the oven and pierce the thickest part of the meat right down to the bone. If the juices that come out are clear, the chicken is perfectly cooked. If they are red or pinkish, give the drumsticks another 5–10 minutes and test them again.
5. Serve the chicken with lime wedges and the salads mentioned above, if you like.

AUTUMN FIG, WALNUT, PROSCIUTTO & PUMPKIN SALAD {SERVES 2}

This salad is a perfect option on those nights when you aren't in the mood for anything too heavy. Rocket has crisp, bitter leaves and is complemented perfectly by the salty prosciutto, the sweet pumpkin and the sticky glaze. If you can't find figs, you can substitute with thinly sliced pear.

1. Bring a saucepan of water to the boil and add the pumpkin. Blanch for 2 minutes then drain and run under cold water to stop the pumpkin overcooking. Set aside.
2. Make the honey and balsamic glaze and simple lemon dressing.
3. Heat the vegetable oil in a medium heavy-based frying pan over a high heat. Add the sliced haloumi and pumpkin. Cook, turning the haloumi once, until it's golden brown on both sides and the pumpkin is tender. Remove the pan from the heat.
4. Meanwhile, combine the figs, rocket, prosciutto, zucchini and walnuts in a large bowl. Drizzle over the simple lemon dressing and toss gently to coat.
5. Divide the haloumi and pumpkin between the serving plates and top with the dressed salad mixture. Drizzle over the honey and balsamic glaze and serve.

⅛ of a butternut pumpkin (squash), cut into 1.5 cm (⅝ inch) dice
1 batch of honey and balsamic glaze (p. 173)
1 batch of simple lemon dressing (p. 115)
1½ tablespoons vegetable oil
100 g (3½ oz) haloumi cheese, cut into 5 mm (¼ inch) slices
2 fresh figs, knobbly tips cut off, sliced into thin wedges
a large handful of baby rocket (arugula)
4 slices of prosciutto, torn
1 zucchini (courgette), outer flesh shaved with a vegetable peeler, core and seeds discarded
2 tablespoons walnut halves, broken into pieces with your hands

THE ANTI-GARDEN SALAD

The very mention of the word salad brings to mind bland green things: boring ol' iceberg lettuce, maybe a bit of cos. Heck, why not throw in some baby spinach? I'll tell you why: There's a new style of salad in town. I call it the anti-garden salad because I'm over the tomato, cucumber and lettuce number that seems to come out at every barbecue. Introduce some thinly sliced or shaved raw vegetables, a few pieces of something crunchy or sweet and a simple dressing, and voila! You've got a cracker of a salad. Just remember to always toss a salad gently with clean hands, not tongs or salad servers, which can bruise your ingredients.

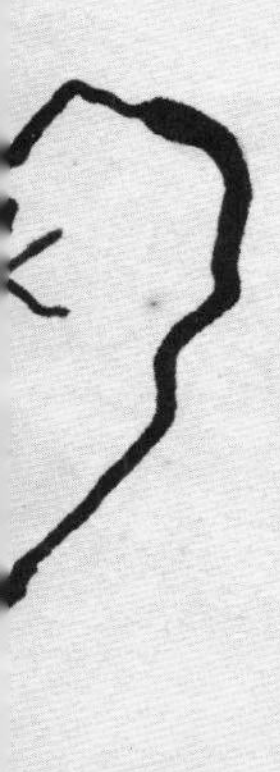

GREAT SALAD INGREDIENTS

The secret to a great vegetable salad isn't using expensive, hard-to-find produce, or tossing all the veggies in your crisper together. I've listed a whole bunch of ingredients on the opposite page. Think of these as building blocks for creating a brilliant salad. Try and use at least one item from each list. If you're stuck for inspiration, you'll find a few of my favourite salads on the following pages.

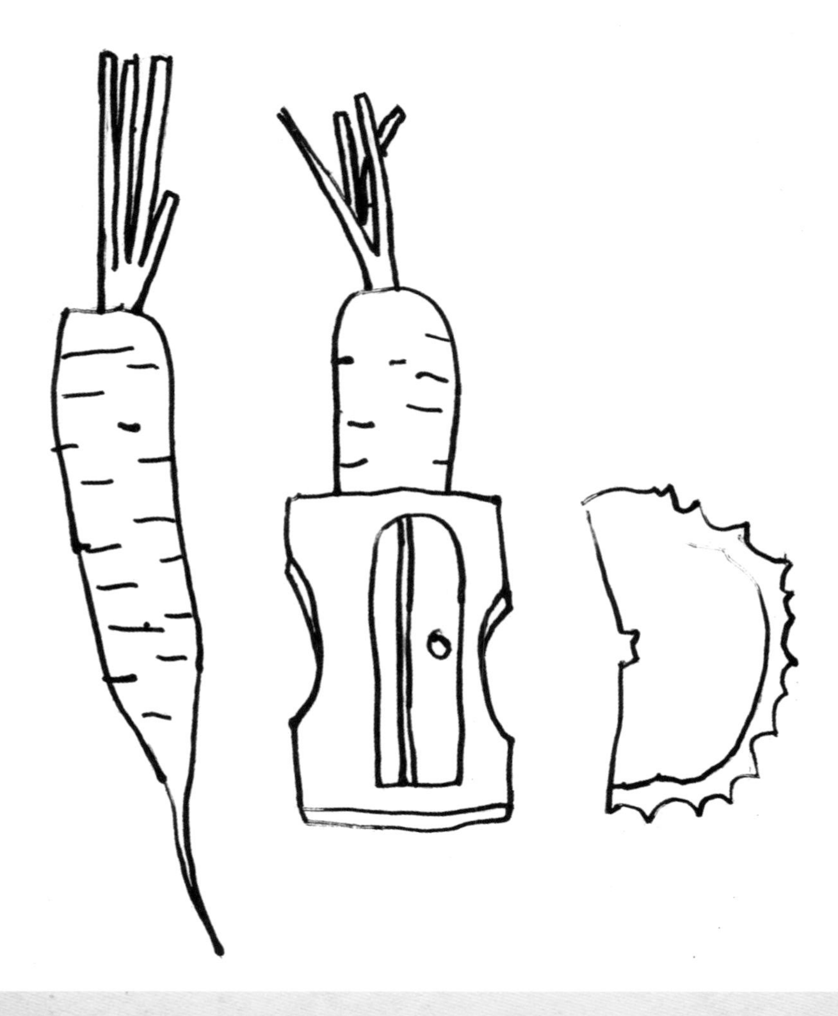

VEGGIES

Zucchini (courgettes), shaved thinly using a peeler
Fennel, shaved thinly using a mandolin
Shallots, spring onions (scallions) or red onions, thinly sliced
Avocados, halved, stone removed, flesh diced
Radishes, thinly sliced
Carrots, shaved thinly using a peeler, or coarsely grated
Tomatoes, diced or sliced
Cucumbers, sliced or peeled into ribbons
Celery stalks, thinly sliced
Beetroot (beet), grated or shaved really thinly using a mandolin
Cabbages, shredded
Radicchio, thinly sliced
Witlof (chicory), thinly sliced
Watercress, leaves picked

A IS FOR APPLE, & OTHER GREAT FRUITS TO USE IN SALADS

Apples, sliced
Oranges, peeled and segmented
Figs, torn or sliced
Pears, sliced
Grapes, left whole or halved
Cherries, pitted and halved
Peaches, halved, stone removed, flesh cut into wedges
Strawberries, hulled and halved or thinly sliced
Raspberries
Dates, chopped
Currants, left whole
Dried cranberries, left whole
Pomegranates, halved and seeds tapped out
Mangoes, halved, stone removed, flesh diced
Plums, halved, stone removed, flesh cut into wedges
Lychees, peeled and halved

NUTS & OTHER CRISPY OR CRUNCHY THINGS

Hazelnuts
Almonds
Cashews
Pistachios
Walnuts
Brazil nuts
Pine nuts
Pepitas (pumpkin seeds)
Sunflower seeds
Toasted breadcrumbs
Crisped-up bacon, prosciutto or pancetta
Sesame seeds
Toasted spices such as cumin, coriander or fennel seeds

HERBS & OTHER SOFT THINGS

Parsley, leaves picked
Mint, leaves picked
Coriander (cilantro), leaves picked
Basil, leaves picked
Chives, snipped
Bean sprouts
Dill, feathery fronds picked
Oregano, leaves picked
Tarragon, leaves picked

HIGH-INTENSITY FLAVOUR

All cheeses (such as feta and parmesan)
Kalamata olives, pitted
Capers, drained and rinsed
Cornichons
Jarred anchovies in oil, drained

DRESSINGS

The general rule of thumb with a European-style dressing is to use a fat (usually oil) and an acidic ingredient (usually vinegar or citrus juice) at a ratio of 2–3 parts fat to 1 part acid. I am a huge fan of the 2:1 ratio because I find the extra acidity in the dressing really makes you want to keep going back for more. So if in doubt, grab whichever oil and acid you have, follow that 2:1 ratio and you'll be fine.

With Asian-style dressings, the goal is to have a balance of sweet, salty and sour, so these are a different kettle of fish sauce altogether (did you see what I did there?).

I have included some of my favourite dressings on these pages and they suit a variety of salads. For each of these dressings, simply put all of their ingredients in a bowl and whisk together. Alternatively, you can put everything in a screw-top jar or container and shake until combined.

SIMPLE LEMON DRESSING

{MAKES ABOUT ¼ CUP}

2 tablespoons extra virgin olive oil
1 tablespoon lemon juice
a pinch of salt, to taste

SIMPLE BALSAMIC DRESSING

{MAKES ABOUT ⅓ CUP}

4 tablespoons extra virgin olive oil
2 tablespoons balsamic vinegar
a pinch of salt, to taste

ORANGE VINAIGRETTE

{MAKES ABOUT ⅓ CUP}

1 tablespoon freshly-squeezed orange juice (squeezed from leftover orange flesh)
1 tablespoon white wine vinegar
2 tablespoons extra virgin olive oil
1 teaspoon dijon mustard
a pinch of salt, to taste

TAHINI, CUMIN & YOGHURT DRESSING

{MAKES ABOUT ⅔ CUP}

95 g (3¼ oz/⅓ cup) thick Greek yoghurt
2 tablespoons lemon juice
1 teaspoon ground cumin
1 teaspoon tahini
1 teaspoon honey
1 teaspoon dijon or wholegrain mustard
1 tablespoon extra virgin olive oil
a pinch of salt, to taste

VIETNAMESE DRESSING

{MAKES ABOUT ⅔ CUP}

4 tablespoons brown sugar
2½ tablespoons fish sauce (available in the Asian section of your supermarket)
2½ tablespoons rice vinegar

MIRIN & SOY DRESSING

{MAKES ABOUT ⅔ CUP}

3 tablespoons mirin (rice wine, available in the Asian section of your supermarket)
1½ tablespoons light soy sauce
2 teaspoons rice vinegar
½ teaspoon sesame oil
1½ teaspoons finely grated fresh ginger

TAMARIND DRESSING

{MAKES ABOUT ⅓ CUP}

2½ tablespoons tamarind paste (available in the Asian section of your supermarket)
2 tablespoons brown sugar
2 tablespoons fish sauce (available in the Asian section of your supermarket)

ZUCCHINI, MINT & FETA SALAD

{SERVES 4}

Raw zucchini is awesome, provided it is shaved nice and thinly. A vegetable peeler makes preparing this salad a piece of cake.

2 zucchini (courgettes)
a small handful of mint leaves, torn
50 g (1¾ oz/⅓ cup) crumbled good-quality feta or goat's cheese
1 batch of simple lemon dressing (p. 115)

Use a vegetable peeler to shave each zucchini into thin slices. Combine in a bowl with the mint leaves and half of the crumbled cheese. At the last minute, add the simple lemon dressing and a pinch of salt, to taste. Toss everything together to combine then scatter over the remaining cheese and serve immediately.

MIXED TOMATO, CAPER, SHALLOT, BASIL & MOZZARELLA SALAD

{SERVES 4}

750 g (1 lb 10 oz) mixed tomatoes (try and find a mix of different sizes and colours)
2 tablespoons baby capers, drained and rinsed
2 red Asian shallots, sliced as thinly as you can
a handful of basil leaves, torn
2 balls of buffalo mozzarella, torn into chunks
1 batch of simple balsamic dressing (p. 115)

1. Cut the tomatoes into a variety of shapes and sizes; some into wedges, some into halves and leave the small ones whole. Place them in a serving bowl with the capers, shallot, basil leaves and mozzarella and toss gently to combine.
2. Drizzle over the simple balsamic dressing right before serving and toss.

RAW BEETROOT, ORANGE & LENTIL SALAD {SERVES 4}

If you have some disposable gloves lying around, now's the time to use them, as beetroot can stain your hands purple. Serve this salad with red meat, salmon or poultry and, if you don't feel like cheese, swap the goat's cheese for plain yoghurt with some horseradish stirred through.

1 beetroot (beet), peeled and coarsely grated
1 x 400 g (14 oz) tin of brown lentils, rinsed and drained
1 batch of orange vinaigrette (p. 115)
2 oranges
50 g (1¾ oz) good-quality goat's cheese (or feta if you like)
a small handful of flat-leaf (Italian) parsley, finely chopped

1. Combine the beetroot in a bowl with the lentils and stir through the orange vinaigrette. Peel the oranges and cut them into segments. Stir half of the oranges through the salad and reserve the rest for serving.
2. Transfer the salad to serving plates or bowls. Top with the remaining orange segments. Tear the goat's cheese into little chunks to distribute over the salad. Sprinkle over the parsley and serve.

SWEETCORN, RED ONION & SMOKED ALMOND SALAD {SERVES 4}

Something about the combination of charred sweetcorn and smoked almonds just works. You could use frozen corn instead of fresh cobs if you like, but the salad won't be quite as good. It works well with Mexican food, especially if accompanied by the Best. Guacamole. Ever. (page 174).

2 cobs of sweetcorn
½ a red onion, finely diced
55 g (2 oz/⅓ cup) smoked almonds, roughly chopped
1 batch of simple lemon dressing (p. 115)
a small handful of coriander (cilantro) leaves, to serve (optional)

1. Heat a barbecue hotplate to high or a large frying pan over a high heat. Cook the cobs of corn in their husks, turning every couple of minutes, until browned and blackened all over. This will take about 15 minutes.
2. Once the corn is cooked, transfer it to a big bowl, cover with plastic wrap and allow it to steam. Let the corn cool for a few minutes, then peel off the husks. Stand the cobs up on a chopping board and use a sharp knife and long, slicing motions to cut all the kernels from the cobs. Allow the kernels to cool a little.
3. Place the corn kernels in a large bowl with the onion, smoked almonds and simple lemon dressing. Stir to combine, top with coriander (if using) and serve.

MOROCCAN CARROT SALAD WITH TAHINI, CUMIN & YOGHURT DRESSING

{SERVES 4}

You may have noticed in the last year or so that supermarkets have been getting on board with the whole multicoloured carrot thing; it's not uncommon to spot purple and white ones in addition to the regulation orange. Apparently, carrots never used to be orange – we actually bred them to be that way. What a clever bunch we are! Anyhow, this salad looks awesome with orange and purple carrots if you can find them, but an all-orange affair is just as tasty.

70 g (2½ oz/½ cup) walnuts, broken up a little by hand
1 batch of tahini, cumin and yoghurt dressing (p. 115)
½ a batch of simple lemon dressing (p. 115)
2 carrots, ideally 1 orange and 1 purple
1 shallot, sliced as thinly as you can
2 tablespoons roughly chopped flat-leaf (Italian) parsley or coriander (cilantro) leaves

1. Preheat the oven to 180°C (350°F/Gas 4). Spread the walnuts onto a baking tray and toast in the oven for 5–10 minutes, or until fragrant. Remove from the oven and allow to cool.
2. Meanwhile, make the tahini, cumin and yoghurt dressing and the lemon dressing, and set both aside.
3. Shave the carrots into long strips about 2 cm (¾ inch) wide using a vegetable peeler. Combine with the shallot and toasted walnuts in a bowl then drizzle over the simple lemon dressing.
4. Spoon the tahini, cumin and yoghurt dressing into the middle of a serving platter. Use a spoon to spread the dressing out. Pile the carrot salad high on top of the dressing. Scatter over the parsley or coriander leaves. Serve immediately.

OUT TO IMPRESS

Food wins people over, it's as simple as that. The recipes in this chapter might require a tiny bit more effort than other recipes in the book, but with greater effort comes greater reward. Want to show off to your mates? Impress a date? Ask someone a favour? If so, cook them one of the following dishes, and then ask them.

BEER & ROSEMARY FOCACCIA

{MAKES 1 FOCACCIA}

Making your own bread is pretty impressive, but the great thing about this focaccia is that it's probably the easiest bread in the world to make. There's no waiting for the dough to prove and certainly no need to knead! (You knew that pun was coming, don't judge me.) Your average bread recipe uses yeast as the raising agent, but in this recipe you can skip all that messing around with yeast and use beer instead. Surprisingly, the bread doesn't have a strong beery taste to it, but it is mighty delicious. This is a great snack by itself or with dips. Make it for friends on movie night, or to eat in front of a footy game.

60 ml (2 fl oz/¼ cup) olive oil, plus extra for greasing and drizzling
450 g (1 lb/3 cups) self-raising flour, plus extra for dusting
1½ tablespoons caster (superfine) sugar
1 x 330 ml (11¼ fl oz/1⅓ cups) bottle of your favourite beer
2 rosemary sprigs, leaves picked
a handful of pitted kalamata olives (optional)
¼ teaspoon salt

1. Preheat the oven to 200°C (400°F/Gas 6). Grease and line a large baking tray with baking paper.
2. In a large bowl, mix the self-raising flour, sugar, olive oil and beer together using a wooden spoon. Mix until a soft, sticky dough forms then transfer the dough to the lined baking tray.
3. Rub flour on your hands to stop the dough sticking to you, then press the dough out with your fingertips into an oval shape about 3 cm (1¼ inches) thick. Brush or drizzle the dough with some olive oil. Push the rosemary and olives (if using) lightly into the dough. Sprinkle the salt evenly over the top then transfer to the oven and bake for 25–30 minutes, or until golden brown.
4. Remove the focaccia from the oven. Allow to cool slightly then slice or tear into chunks and serve while it's still warm.

HALOUMI, ASPARAGUS & POMEGRANATE QUINOA WITH CHUNKY PARSLEY SAUCE {SERVES 2}

This is one of those great recipes that looks more complicated than it actually is. It's great on its own, or as a side with roast lamb or grilled mushrooms or zucchini (courgettes). Bash out the seeds from the leftover pomegranate half and scatter them on your muesli, fruit salads or in a punch. You can substitute dried cranberries for the pomegranate seeds when they are out of season.

1. Place the quinoa in a small saucepan, cover with about 1 cup of hot water and bring to the boil. Reduce the heat to a simmer and cook for 13–15 minutes, or until tender.
2. Meanwhile, make the parsley sauce by combining the parsley, almonds, garlic and lemon juice in a small food processor with a pinch of salt. Blend until well chopped then add the extra virgin olive oil and stir to combine.
3. Heat the canola oil in a large non-stick frying pan over a high heat. Add the haloumi slices and cook, turning once, until they are golden brown on both sides. Remove the haloumi and add the asparagus to the pan. Cook for 1–2 minutes, tossing them in the pan so they cook on all sides. Remove from the heat once the asparagus is bright green but still a little crunchy.
4. Use a wooden spoon to repeatedly hit the back of the pomegranate half until the seeds fall out. Discard any white pith.
5. Drain any leftover liquid from the quinoa and transfer it to a bowl. Stir through the pomegranate seeds and asparagus. Divide the quinoa between two serving plates and top with the slices of golden haloumi.
6. Serve with dollops of the parsley sauce on top.

HALOUMI & POMEGRANATE QUINOA

65 g (2⅓ oz/⅓ cup) white quinoa
1 tablespoon canola oil
100 g (3½ oz) haloumi cheese, thickly sliced
6–8 spears (1 bunch) of asparagus, woody ends snapped off, stems sliced into 3 cm (1¼ inch) pieces, tips left whole
seeds from ½ a pomegranate

CHUNKY PARSLEY SAUCE

a large handful of flat-leaf (Italian) parsley
2 tablespoons slivered almonds
1 garlic clove, sliced
1½ tablespoons lemon juice
60 ml (2 fl oz/¼ cup) extra virgin olive oil

BRAISED CHICKEN & GREEN MANGO SALAD {SERVES 4}

I made this to sell at our Sprout stall at an Adelaide festival called CheeseFest – a two-day celebration of all things cheese. 'But there's no cheese in this recipe!' I hear you cry in outrage. I know. That was kind of the point: to offer a lighter alternative to the delicious, rich cheeses people were trying. It must have worked. We sold over 400 salads in two days!

BRAISED CHICKEN

1 x 1.5 kg (3 lb 5 oz) free-range chicken, rinsed
250 ml (9 fl oz/1 cup) Chinese rice wine
125 ml (4 fl oz/½ cup) soy sauce
4 spring onions (scallions)
a large knob of ginger, thickly sliced on an angle
6 garlic cloves

GREEN MANGO SALAD

1 batch of Vietnamese dressing (p. 115)
1 long red chilli, seeded and thinly sliced
20 g (¾ oz/¼ cup) shredded coconut
6 spring onions (scallions), green and whites thinly sliced
1 carrot, finely grated or julienned
a large handful of bean sprouts
a large handful of mint leaves, torn
a large handful of coriander (cilantro) leaves, torn
90 g (3¼ oz/1 cup) grated green mango (or green papaya or granny smith apple)
35 g (1¼ oz/¼ cup) roasted peanuts, coarsely chopped
2 tablespoons fried shallots

1. Combine the chicken and all of its braising ingredients in a saucepan large enough to fit the whole chicken. Add just enough water to cover. Bring to the boil over a high heat, then immediately turn down to a low heat and simmer very (very!) gently — just the odd bubble should emerge — for 1¼ hours, or until the chicken is just cooked through. Once the time is up, move the chicken to a chopping board and slice open the thickest part of the thigh to check it is cooked through (piping hot flesh and no trace of pink in the juices).
2. Meanwhile, make your Vietnamese dressing and mix through half of the sliced chilli.
3. Heat a small frying pan over a high heat. Add the coconut to the dry pan and toast, stirring and tossing around constantly, until light golden brown and fragrant. Transfer to a small bowl until ready to use.
4. Allow the chicken to cool down enough to handle, then shred the meat with two forks, discarding any skin and bones. Strain its cooking broth and freeze to use for soup another day.
5. Combine most of the remaining chilli, the spring onion, carrot, bean sprouts, mint, coriander, mango, peanuts, fried shallots and toasted coconut in a large bowl. Mix through the shredded chicken meat, pour over the dressing and toss gently to combine. Top with more chilli if you like things spicy. Serve immediately.

SPANISH MUSSELS {SERVES 2}

I spent a day at a mussel farm in the seafood capital of South Australia, Port Lincoln. I asked the farmer what his favourite way to eat mussels was and he said with chorizo and tomato. You can't argue with a man who produces tonnes of mussels every year! Mussels have a somewhat fancy reputation, but they are actually very affordable and, because of the way they're farmed, they're also incredibly sustainable and eco-friendly. So if you've never tried cooking mussels before, now's your chance. They're so simple and quick to cook; that's probably why so many restaurants have them on the menu!

1 tablespoon canola oil
1 red onion, halved and thinly sliced
1 chorizo sausage, thinly sliced
1 long red chilli, seeded and thinly sliced (optional)
2 garlic cloves
2 teaspoons smoked paprika
1 x 400 g (14 oz) tin of chopped tomatoes
125 ml (4 fl oz/½ cup) good-quality chicken stock or water
1 kg (2 lb 4 oz) mussels, scrubbed clean and beards removed (sometimes these are called pot-ready mussels)
a handful of flat-leaf (Italian) parsley, roughly chopped
crusty bread, to serve

1. Heat a large heavy-based pot over a high heat. Add the canola oil then the onion and chorizo. Cook for 2–3 minutes, or until the onion and chorizo turn golden and smell delicious. Add the chilli (if using), garlic and paprika and cook for a further minute before adding the tomatoes. Simmer for 10–15 minutes, stirring occasionally, or until the tomatoes darken in colour.
2. Add the chicken stock or water, bring to the boil, then add the mussels. Cover with a lid and steam for 3–5 minutes, shaking the pot occasionally, until all of the mussels open. If one or two don't open, don't stress. They aren't bad mussels like many people think (I've been assured by the mussel grower!). Prise them open carefully with a small knife, and if they look good, go for it. Divide between serving bowls, top with the chopped parsley and serve immediately with crusty bread.

ROSEMARY CHICKEN WITH GRAPE SALAD

{SERVES 4 AS A LIGHT LUNCH OR 2–3 PARTICULARLY PECKISH FOLK}

Cooking chicken thighs in a hot pan then basting them with a little butter and rosemary gives you that amazing roast-chicken flavour that normally takes over an hour to achieve with a whole bird. Pair with some salty bacon, crisp sweet grapes, crunchy walnuts and a creamy dressing and you're ticking every box. Just make sure you serve some toasted sourdough to soak up any leftover dressing!

1. Make the dressings. Put the simple lemon dressing into a large salad bowl then pile the other salad ingredients on top and put aside without tossing.
2. Heat a heavy-based non-stick frying pan over a high heat. Add ½ a tablespoon of the canola oil, then the bacon and cook until very crispy on both sides. Remove to a paper towel to drain and set aside. Wipe out the pan.
3. Place the chicken thighs between two sheets of baking paper and use a meat mallet or heavy saucepan to pound them to an even thickness. Add the remaining canola oil to the pan, then the chicken. Season with salt and pepper. Cook for 3–4 minutes, turn over, and cook for another 2 minutes. Turn down the heat a little and add the butter and rosemary to the pan. Use a spoon to baste each chicken thigh several times. Once the chicken is just cooked (no sign of pink in the juices) remove the thighs to a clean chopping board and discard the rosemary.
4. Smear some tahini dressing in circles on four serving plates. Slice each chicken thigh into seven or eight pieces on a slight angle. Divide between the plates and top each serving with a rasher of crispy bacon.
5. Quickly toss the salad then divide between the plates and serve immediately with the slices of toasted sourdough.

ROSEMARY CHICKEN

2 tablespoons canola oil
4 rashers of bacon, sliced 5 mm (¼ inch) thick
4 boneless, skinless free-range chicken thighs
1½ tablespoons butter
2 rosemary sprigs

GRAPE SALAD

2 batches of tahini, cumin and yoghurt dressing (p. 115)
1 batch of simple lemon dressing (p. 115)
270 g (9½ oz/1½ cups) green or red seedless grapes, halved lengthways
1 Lebanese (short) cucumber, halved, lengthways, seeded and thinly sliced
2 shallots, sliced as thinly as you can
a handful of chopped flat-leaf (Italian) parsley leaves
a small handful of snipped chives
60 g (2¼ oz/½ cup) walnuts, roughly crushed

4 lightly toasted slices of sourdough bread, to serve

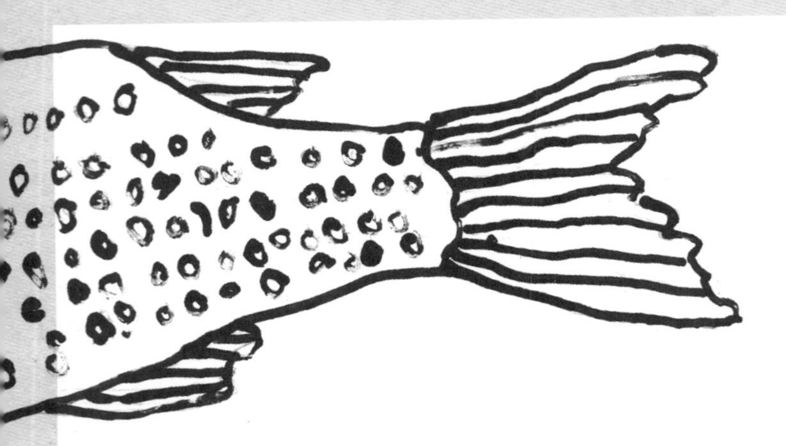

FISH IN A BAG

You may have eaten fish like this in a restaurant before. It is likely they referred to the technique as en papillote (French for 'in parchment') as it sounds a heck of a lot fancier than fish cooked in a bag. Cooking the fish wrapped up in a parcel of foil and baking paper works in two ways: it locks in all the moisture, so you're guaranteed juicy, tender fish every time, and it also helps any flavours you've added to the parcel to penetrate right through the fish. If you're nervous about your fish-cooking abilities, try one of my favourite foolproof recipes on the next pages.

COCONUT WHITE FISH WITH MANGO SALAD & NAHM JIM {SERVES 2}

I love the combination of sweet mango with delicately cooked fish and the nahm jim dressing, which is bold enough to knock your socks off. The kaffir lime leaves (or lemon leaves) are well worth tracking down as the aroma and flavour they impart is something special.

FISH PARCELS

60 ml (2 fl oz/¼ cup) coconut milk
1½ teaspoons fish sauce
1 teaspoon brown sugar
3 kaffir lime leaves, torn (you can substitute with leaves from a lemon tree)
1 lemongrass stem, twisted, bruised and sliced on an angle
2 x 150 g (5½ oz) firm-fleshed white fish fillets, such as snapper or barramundi

MANGO SALAD & NAHM JIM

1 batch of green nahm jim dressing (p. 179)
1 Lebanese (short) cucumber, seeded and diced
1 mango, flesh removed and diced
1 shallot, thinly sliced
a small handful of fresh mint leaves, torn
a small handful of coriander (cilantro) leaves, torn

1. Preheat the oven to 190°C (375°F/Gas 5).
2. Combine the coconut milk, fish sauce, brown sugar, lime leaves and lemongrass in a small bowl.
3. Lay two large pieces of foil approx. 25 x 35 cm (10 x 14 inches) on your work bench. Place a similar-sized sheet of baking paper over each piece of foil then lay a fish fillet in the middle of each sheet of paper. Pour the coconut mixture all over each fillet then scatter over the slices of lemongrass.
4. Now for the fun bit: fold the long ends of the foil up over the fish and fold together neatly. Fold up both other sides of the foil to seal. Place the parcels on a baking tray and bake for between 12–18 minutes, depending on the thickness of the fish.
5. Meanwhile, make the nahm jim.
6. Combine the cucumber, mango, shallot, mint and coriander in a bowl.
7. Remove the foil and paper parcels from the oven, and cut open the foil (mind the steam). Carefully transfer the parcels to your serving plates. Divide the salad between the plates, drizzle over the nahm jim then serve immediately.

SALMON WITH CHINESE FLAVOURS

{SERVES 2}

Themis and I cooked this for a Sprout class where several of the people were dubious about whether or not they liked fish. Upon giving it a try, every one of them ate their whole parcel! I hope your guest enjoys this dish as much as they did.

FISH PARCELS

60 ml (2 fl oz/¼ cup) Chinese rice wine (or you can substitute with sake or dry sherry)
1½ tablespoons oyster sauce
1½ tablespoons soy sauce
1½ teaspoons finely grated fresh ginger
¼ teaspoon sesame oil
3 spring onions (scallions), thinly sliced on an angle
½ a red chilli, seeded and thinly sliced
a handful of coriander (cilantro) leaves
2 x 150 g (5½ oz) salmon (or ocean trout) fillets
¾ teaspoon Chinese five-spice

GREENS

2 teaspoons vegetable oil
2 garlic cloves, thinly sliced
a large handful of snow peas (mangetout)
3 bok choy (pak choy) or other leafy greens, quartered
2 tablespoons oyster sauce
¼ teaspoon sesame oil

1. Preheat the oven to 200°C (400°F/Gas 6) (fan-forced). Put the rice wine, oyster and soy sauces, ginger and sesame oil in a small bowl and whisk to combine.
2. Lay two large pieces of foil (approx. 25 × 35 cm/10 × 14 inches) on your work bench. Place a similar-sized sheet of baking paper over each piece of foil then divide the spring onions, chilli and coriander between them. Spread the ingredients out a little to make a bed for the fish fillets. Place a piece of fish on top of each bed, rub each fillet with five-spice then spoon over the soy dressing.
3. Carefully fold the foil around each piece of fish to form two airtight parcels. Transfer the parcels to a baking tray, place in the oven and cook for between 10–15 minutes, depending on the thickness of the fish.
4. While the fish is in the oven, prepare the greens. Heat the vegetable oil in a large frying pan or wok over a high heat. Add the garlic, then the snow peas and bok choy, stirring and tossing everything constantly to keep it moving around the pan. Add the oyster sauce and a splash of water to create some steam. Continue to toss everything around the pan for about 3–4 more minutes, adding a tiny bit more water if the pan becomes too dry. When the vegetables are bright green but still have some crunch, divide them between two serving plates and drizzle with the sesame oil.
5. Remove the parcels from the oven and carefully put one on each plate next to the vegetables. Cut them open (mind the steam) and get stuck in!

SALMON & SOBA NOODLE SALAD

{SERVES 2 AS A MAIN OR 4–6 AS PART OF A BANQUET}

This is a really healthy dish that is great on its own, or served on the table as part of a meal.

- 1 batch of mirin and soy dressing (p. 115)
- 1 x 90 g (3¼ oz) packet of dried soba noodles
- a large handful of snow peas (mangetout)
- 1½ tablespoons vegetable oil, plus extra for drizzling
- 2 x 150 g (5½ oz) salmon fillets, skin on
- 5 shiittake mushrooms, sliced (or you can use Swiss brown, enoki or oyster mushrooms)
- 1 Lebanese (short) cucumber
- a small handful of coriander (cilantro) leaves
- ½ teaspoon sesame seeds

1. Make the mirin and soy dressing.
2. Blanch the soba noodles in a saucepan of boiling water according to the packet directions. Add the snow peas for the last 2 minutes of cooking then drain and refresh under a little cold water. Drain again. Toss the noodles in a little drizzle of vegetable oil to stop them sticking together.
3. Meanwhile, heat a non-stick frying pan over a high heat. Add the oil then the salmon, skin side down, and cook for 5–7 minutes, turning once halfway through. Remove the salmon from the heat and allow to cool slightly.
   Use a fork to flake the salmon into large chunks.
4. Put the same pan you used for the salmon back over a high heat, add the mushrooms and cook for 2–3 minutes, or until tender.
5. Coarsely grate or julienne the cucumber, then use paper towel to blot as much water from the cucumber as possible.
6. Combine the noodles, cucumber and coriander in a bowl. Stir through the mushrooms and most of the salmon.
7. Pour over the dressing and gently mix everything together. Pile onto a serving platter, top with the remaining salmon and sprinkle over the sesame seeds. Serve immediately.

HONEY-GLAZED DUCK WITH PEACH, SMOKED ALMOND & BABY COS SALAD

{SERVES 2}

This recipe is one I cooked with my mate Michael Weldon at a cooking demonstration. It was one of those days where everything went wrong. We lost power, so we couldn't get our pans hot. That also meant we lost our microphones, so we were yelling to the audience. I'm not quite sure how we pulled it together, but the dish tasted great. I implore you to give it a go, even if you've never cooked duck before. Duck breasts are available from most butchers.

HONEY-GLAZED DUCK

2 duck breasts, skin on
2 tablespoons honey

BABY COS SALAD

2 baby cos (romaine) lettuces, stalks removed, leaves separated
2 tablespoons smoked almonds, roughly chopped
2 small peaches, stones removed, sliced
1 Lebanese (short) cucumber, halved lengthways and sliced
1 shallot, peeled and sliced as thinly as you can
8 tarragon sprigs, leaves picked (optional)
¼ bunch of watercress, leaves picked (optional)
2 tablespoons lemon juice
1 tablespoon extra virgin olive oil

1. Place the duck breasts, skin side down, in a cold medium non-stick frying pan. Place over a medium heat and allow the pan to come slowly up to heat and start to render some of the duck fat out. Increase the heat and once the skin is deep golden brown and nice and crispy (this takes about 4–8 minutes), turn the duck over and cook for a further 3–4 minutes, or until cooked to your liking. (I like medium-cooked duck, which still has a touch of pink in the middle.) Season with salt and freshly ground black pepper then remove from the pan to rest, skin side up.
2. Combine the cos leaves, smoked almonds, peach, cucumber, shallot and the tarragon and watercress (if using) in a large salad bowl.
3. While the duck is resting, pour away most of the fat from the frying pan then place it back over a medium heat. Add 2 tablespoons of water and use a wooden spoon or plastic-coated tongs to scrape any stuck-on bits from the bottom of the pan. Add the honey and stir to combine with the pan juices.
4. Quickly remove from the heat and add 1 tablespoon of the lemon juice.
5. Slice the duck. Drizzle the remaining tablespoon of lemon juice and the extra virgin olive oil over the salad, then season to taste and toss to combine.
6. Pour the warm honey glaze over the duck and salad and serve immediately.

SPICE-CRUSTED PORK LOIN WITH APPLE CIDER GLAZE & FIGS

{SERVES 4}

Pork sometimes cops a bad rap; people think that it's fatty (pork loin is no fattier than chicken!) and that you can get sick if you don't cook the heck out of it. You do need to cook minced (ground) pork all the way through, but whole cuts can actually be cooked so they are a little pink in the middle for a juicier, more tender result.

The sweet and sour apple cider glaze and figs work perfectly with the pork, but you definitely need the bitter leafy vegetables to balance out the dish. Make this into a heartier meal by serving with the mac 'n' cheese on page 80, some mashed potato or even a potato salad with lots of wholegrain mustard stirred through.

1 tablespoon coriander seeds
1 tablespoon fennel seeds
¼ teaspoon salt
4 x 150 g (5½ oz) pieces of pork loin or fillet
2 tablespoons canola oil
1 batch of simple lemon dressing (p. 115)
4 large handfuls of bitter leafy salad vegetables, such as rocket (arugula), a head of radicchio or witlof (chicory)
6 fresh figs, cut into wedges

APPLE CIDER GLAZE

1 x 330 ml (11¼ fl oz/1⅓ cups) bottle of dry apple cider
250 ml (9 fl oz/1 cup) clear apple juice

1. Combine the cider, apple juice and a pinch of salt in a medium saucepan and bring to the boil. Continue to boil until the mixture has reduced by three-quarters and has the consistency of a thin syrup. Remove from the heat.
2. Toast the coriander and fennel seeds in a hot, dry frying pan over a medium heat for 1 minute, or until fragrant. Use a mortar and pestle or a small food processor to crush them to a powder with the salt. If you don't have either of those, you can wrap them in a clean tea towel (dish towel) with the salt and give them a good bash with something heavy.
3. Rub the crushed spices all over the pork.
4. Heat the canola oil in a large non-stick frying pan over a medium–high heat. Add the pork and cook for 3–4 minutes on each side, or until the pork is a deep golden brown and cooked to your liking. Remove to a chopping board and rest for around 3–4 minutes.
5. Drizzle the simple lemon dressing over your chosen bitter leafy vegetable and serve with the pork, figs and a drizzle of the apple cider glaze.

WHITE CHOCOLATE MOUSSE WITH BALSAMIC & BLACK PEPPER BERRIES

{SERVES 4}

Balsamic vinegar and black pepper with strawberries? All together?! You may think I'm barking mad, but I promise you it tastes great. The acidity from the vinegar and hint of spice from the pepper brings out the best flavour from the strawberries, and the white chocolate mousse is the perfect sweet and creamy sidekick. A little crumble for crunch completes the picture, but if you can't be bothered, a handful of flaked almonds would be almost as good.

1. Make the simple crumble and set aside.
2. Hull the strawberries (cut off their green tops) then slice, halve or quarter them and put them in a medium bowl. Add the icing sugar, balsamic vinegar and a good few twists of black pepper then gently stir to combine. Set aside while you make the white chocolate mousse.
3. Use an electric mixer with a whisk attachment to whisk the cream and vanilla bean paste together until firm peaks start to form (be careful not to over whisk).
4. Melt the chocolate slowly in a heatproof bowl over a saucepan of gently simmering water (make sure the water isn't touching the bottom of the bowl). Stir gently with a metal spoon until melted. Alternatively, you can melt the chocolate in a microwave-safe container in the microwave on full power in 10-second bursts, stirring gently after each burst until smooth.
5. Whisk the egg yolk into the melted chocolate, then whisk in the hot water and fold the chocolate mixture through the cream. Divide this mixture between four small bowls or pretty glasses, and place in the fridge for at least 1 hour.
6. Before serving, top with the balsamic and black pepper strawberries, any syrup from the bottom of the strawberry bowl and the simple crumble.

1 batch of simple crumble, to serve (p. 182)

BALSAMIC & BLACK PEPPER BERRIES

500 g (1 lb 2 oz/3⅓ cups/2 punnets) strawberries
2 tablespoons icing (confectioners') sugar
2 tablespoons balsamic vinegar
6–8 good turns of the black pepper mill

WHITE CHOCOLATE MOUSSE

250 ml (9 fl oz/1 cup) thickened (whipping) cream
1 teaspoon vanilla bean paste
125 g (4½ oz) white chocolate, roughly chopped
1 free-range egg yolk
1 tablespoon hot water

CHERRY FOOL {SERVES 4}

Cherries, to me, are pretty special. Unlike some fruits and veg that are available all year round, we must wait until summer is near for the short cherry season. I like to buy more than I need, remove all the pits from the extras and freeze them in snap-lock bags. Frozen cherries are great in drinks, baked desserts or as a substitute for raspberries in the instant sorbet on page 85.

- 300 g (10½ oz/2 cups) pitted cherries, halved
- 150 g (5½ oz/⅔ cup) caster (superfine) sugar
- 1 tablespoon lemon juice
- 375 ml (13 fl oz/1½ cups) thickened (whipping) cream
- 2 teaspoons vanilla bean paste
- 1–2 teaspoons rosewater, to taste (optional)
- 2 tablespoons roughly chopped pistachios (optional)

1. Place half the cherries in a medium frying pan over a medium heat (reserve the remaining cherries for serving). Add the caster sugar and lemon juice, and crush lightly with a fork.
2. Stir gently until the sugar has dissolved in the lemon and cherry juices. Simmer for 4–5 minutes, or until the cherries are soft and the juice mixture is syrupy. Leave longer for thicker syrup, if desired. Transfer to a bowl and refrigerate until cold.
3. Once the cherries and their syrup are cold, whip the cream, vanilla bean paste and rosewater (if using) until firm peaks form. Fold the whipped cream through the cherries and syrup and add the reserved fresh cherries.
4. Spoon into pretty glasses and serve topped with the chopped pistachios (if using).

GRILLED BROWN SUGAR PINEAPPLE, HAZELNUT CRUMBLE & KIRSTY'S BRANDIED CUSTARD

{SERVES 2}

This dessert is quick and easy to adapt. I've chosen to use pineapple because they were at their best as I was writing this book, but you can also try this dessert with peaches, figs or bananas. You may have some custard left over. If so, just refrigerate and reheat it another night.

1 batch of Kirsty's custard (p. 184)
2 tablespoons brandy

HAZELNUT CRUMBLE

½ a batch of simple crumble (p. 182)
3 tablespoons hazelnuts, halved

GRILLED PINEAPPLE

½ a pineapple (that's been halved lengthways)
2 tablespoons brown sugar

1. Make Kirsty's custard. Stir in the brandy and put aside until serving.
2. Make the simple crumble. Put the hazelnuts in a dry frying pan over a medium heat and move them around for a minute or so until lightly toasted then roughly chop them and stir them through the crumble. Transfer the mixture to a small bowl, ready for serving.
3. Preheat the grill (broiler) to high. Cut each end off the pineapple half to give you a flat surface to stand it on. Carefully slice away any skin and discard it. Halve the pineapple across then lay the pieces on a baking tray. Sprinkle the brown sugar evenly all over then place under the grill for about 2–4 minutes, or until the sugar has melted and caramelised.
4. Serve immediately with a few spoonfuls of warm custard and a sprinkle of the hazelnut crumble.

CARAMELISED STOUT PANNA COTTA

{SERVES 4}

This recipe does take a little time to make, but I promise you it is delicious. In fact, it has to be one of my most frequently requested recipes – I've literally had strangers walk up to me on the street and ask me for this recipe! Something about salt, caramel and bitter stout in one mouthful makes it a winning combination with stout lovers and haters alike.

- 75 g (2¾ oz/⅓ cup) caster (superfine) sugar
- 350 ml (12 fl oz) thickened (whipping) cream
- 80 ml (2½ fl oz/⅓ cup) of your favourite stout (to taste, use less if desired)
- ¼ heaped teaspoon salt
- 2 gold strength gelatine leaves, soaked in cold water (available online, and from providores or specialty food stores)
- 2 tablespoons cocoa nibs, to serve (available from health food stores)
- 35 g (1¼ oz/¼ cup) hazelnuts, halved, to serve

5-MINUTE CHOCOLATE MOUSSE

- 250 ml (9 fl oz/1 cup) thickened (whipping) cream
- 200 g (7 oz) dark chocolate, roughly chopped

1. Bring the caster sugar and about 3 tablespoons of water to the boil over a high heat in a medium heavy-based saucepan. If the sugar flicks up the side of the pan, use a wet pastry brush to brush it back down. When the mixture starts to smoke, and turns a dark caramel colour, stop the cooking by placing the pan in a bowl of cold water.
2. Add the cream, return the pan to a medium heat and simmer gently, whisking constantly, until combined. Whisk in the stout and salt, and simmer for a minute.
3. Squeeze the excess water out of the gelatine leaves, and whisk into the cream mixture until completely dissolved. Transfer the mixture to a bowl and chill over a larger bowl of ice water until the mixture cools to room temperature.
4. Divide between four serving glasses then refrigerate for 2 hours, or until set but still a little bit wobbly.
5. Place the cream for the chocolate mousse in a large bowl and use a hand-held electric whisk to whisk the cream to firm peaks.
6. Melt the chocolate in a heatproof bowl over a small saucepan of simmering water (make sure the water is not touching the bottom of the bowl). Stir gently with a metal spoon until melted, then remove from the heat, allow to cool for a minute then pour into the whipped cream, whisking gently the whole time. Don't whisk too much once the mixture has combined or it may split.
7. To serve, remove the panna cottas from the fridge. Top with a spoonful of chocolate mousse and the cocoa nibs and hazelnuts. Serve immediately.

PASSIONFRUIT PARFAIT {SERVES 4}

A parfait is sort of like ice cream, but it is frozen in a pan or mould rather than churned. This is a cracker of a base recipe and can be flavoured with spices or citrus zest for added flavour, or perhaps folded through almonds or pistachios for crunch. I've chosen to use passionfruit because the acidity cuts through the creaminess of the other ingredients perfectly. Choose passionfruit that feels heavy for its size; this means it's bursting with pulp.

200 ml (7 fl oz) thickened (whipping) cream
2 teaspoons vanilla bean paste
8 passionfruit, 4 of them halved and their pulp scooped out
3 free-range egg whites
75 g (2¾ oz/⅓ cup) caster (superfine) sugar
2 mangoes

1. Line a 12 × 22 cm (4½ × 8½ inch) loaf (bar) tin with plastic wrap so it hangs over the sides of the tin.
2. Use an electric mixer with a whisk attachment to whip the thickened cream and vanilla bean paste to soft peaks in a large bowl. Gently stir in the pulp of 4 passionfruit until combined. Clean the whisk, then place the egg whites in a separate large bowl and whisk until soft peaks form. Slowly add the sugar with the mixer running and continue whisking until a stiff, shiny meringue is achieved. Fold the passionfruit cream into the meringue.
3. Spoon the mixture into the loaf tin and smooth with a spatula or knife. Cover with the overhanging plastic wrap then freeze for 4 hours, or overnight, until firm.
4. Once the parfait has set, cut the cheeks off the mangoes. Discard the stones. Scoop out the flesh and slice into strips.
5. Turn the parfait out onto a chopping board, remove the plastic wrap and cut into slices. Divide these slices between four plates. Arrange some mango next to each serving. Halve the remaining passionfruit, spoon over their pulp and serve immediately.

GET YOUR BAKE ON (NOT BACON!)

Crank your oven. Get your oven mitts at the ready. Sort yourself out with a spatula, whisk and electric beaters. Measuring cups and spoons? You betcha. This chapter is all about my favourite baked goods. If you're already a baking type, you'll love it. If not, now is a great time to start.

SALTED DIRTY BLONDIES {MAKES 16}

Oh my gosh, these are so delicious! I'm eating one as I write this and I'm getting crumbs everywhere but I don't care. Whatever you are doing right now, stop and get whichever ingredients you don't have on this list and make these. Go on! But please don't over-bake them; they are best when they're still a little soft and gooey in the middle. Yum.

- 180 g (6¼ oz) unsalted butter, melted, plus extra for greasing
- 285 g (just over 10 oz/1½ cups, lightly packed) brown sugar
- 2 free-range eggs
- 2 teaspoons vanilla bean paste or natural vanilla extract
- 2 teaspoons instant coffee granules (optional)
- 225 g (8 oz/1½ cups) plain (all-purpose) flour
- sea salt flakes
- 65 g (2⅓ oz/½ cup) slivered almonds
- 140 g (5 oz/1 cup) white chocolate melts

1. Preheat the oven to 190°C (375°F/Gas 5). Grease and line a 20 cm (8 inch) square baking tin.
2. Mix the melted butter and brown sugar together in a large bowl. Beat in the eggs, one at a time, then the vanilla and coffee (if using). Stir in the flour and a big pinch of sea salt. Carefully fold in the almonds and the white chocolate melts.
3. Spoon the mixture into the baking tin. Scatter a couple of pinches of salt over the top of the blondie mixture.
4. Bake for 17–25 minutes, or until the blondie just comes away from the sides of the tin and the middle still has a slight wobble when you shake the tin.
5. Remove from the oven, sprinkle over one final pinch of salt and allow to cool for at least 30 minutes (I know, torture!) before carefully turning out and cutting into 5 cm (2 inch) squares. Hoof in.

20-MINUTE PLUM TART {SERVES 2}

This open tart is a great last-minute dessert. The pastry puffs up around the plums and looks a treat and, because you're using puff pastry, you don't need to blind bake like you do with some fruit tarts. I always have puff pastry and ice cream in the freezer, so this dessert is never far away. It also works well with peaches, apricots or figs.

1 square sheet (27 cm/10¾ inches) of frozen puff pastry, thawed
2 plums, stones removed, flesh cut into wedges
1 free-range egg, lightly beaten
1 tablespoon brown sugar
¼ teaspoon ground cinnamon
2 scoops of vanilla ice cream, to serve

1. Preheat the oven to 190°C (375°F/Gas 5). Line a baking tray big enough to hold the sheet of pastry with baking paper. Remove any packaging from the pastry and lay it in the centre of the tray.
2. Carefully arrange the wedges of one plum in a line down the centre of the pastry sheet so they're slightly overlapping. Place the remaining wedges next to the first wedges so you have two rows. Use a paring knife to score lines marking a rectangle directly around the plum wedges. Cut a rectangle 2 cm (¾ inch) around the plum and discard the pastry trimmings; you should be left with a pastry rectangle with a 2 cm (¾ inch) border, encasing a rectangle of plum wedges.
3. Paint the pastry border with the beaten egg. Sprinkle the brown sugar over the plums then transfer to the oven and bake for 15–20 minutes, or until the pastry is golden and the plums have softened.
4. Remove the tart from the oven and serve immediately with some vanilla ice cream.

STRAWBERRY SHORTCAKE {SERVES 6}

Here's a classic please-everyone recipe. Who doesn't love strawberries and cream, right? I much prefer rich, buttery shortbread in this recipe to sponge, which some strawberry shortcake recipes use. Swapping the cream for crème pat (see page 182) is a delicious alternative.

- 100 g (3½ oz) unsalted butter, plus extra for greasing
- 100 g (3½ oz/½ cup, lightly packed) brown sugar
- 1 free-range egg
- 150 g (5½ oz/1 cup) self-raising flour, sifted
- 310 ml (10¾ fl oz/1¼ cups) thickened (whipping) cream
- 1 teaspoon vanilla bean paste
- 2 tablespoons icing (confectioners') sugar
- 250 g (9 oz/1⅔ cups/1 punnet) strawberries, hulled

1. Preheat the oven to 190°C (375°F/Gas 5). Grease and line two 20 cm (8 inch) springform cake tins with baking paper. In the bowl of an electric stand mixer, cream together the butter and sugar until creamy. Alternatively, use hand-held electric beaters. Beat in the egg until combined then use a spatula to fold in the flour. Divide the mixture evenly between the tins. It should be very thick, like a biscuit dough, so use your hands to gently press and push it out until the mixture covers the surface of each tin.
2. Bake for 13–16 minutes, or until golden brown. Remove the tins from the oven and allow to cool for a few minutes. Open the springform tins then carefully transfer the shortbreads to a wire rack and allow to cool.
3. Meanwhile, place the cream in the bowl of the electric mixer with the vanilla bean paste and icing sugar and beat until firm peaks form. Halve the strawberries and set aside.
4. Once the bases have cooled, place one of the shortbreads on a serving plate then spread a third of the cream mixture on top. Arrange the strawberries all over the cream, reserving a handful for the top. Top with the second shortbread, and cover with the rest of the cream. Pile the reserved strawberries in the middle and serve.

TWO SIMPLE SOUFFLÉS

That's right, I called them simple soufflés. An oxymoron, right? I have taught people how to make a few soufflés at my Sprout classes, and there's often a look of panic the minute the S-bomb is mentioned. But I promise they are not as difficult to make as you might think. If you follow my tips below, you'll end up with a great soufflé.

1. Firstly, use canola spray oil to get a light but even coating of oil on the inside of your ramekins or soufflé moulds. Then add caster (superfine) sugar to one of the ramekins (any amount, but use more than you think you need) and rotate it until a thin, even layer of sugar coats the inside surface. Tip the excess sugar into the next ramekin and repeat. This sugar coating helps the soufflé rise evenly, and forms a delicious crust.
2. You need to make a quality meringue. Make sure no traces of egg yolk are present in the whites, and that your bowl and beaters or whisk are very clean and dry. Whisk your egg whites until soft peaks form, then sprinkle over sugar while still whisking until firm peaks form. To test the meringues, turn your electric mixer off and raise the whisks above the bowl. There should be a stiff peak left behind in the egg white.
3. When mixing the beaten egg whites into your flavouring (raspberry purée or passionfruit pulp in these recipes), fold in one-third of the egg first until well combined, then carefully fold in the remaining two-thirds to avoid knocking too much air out. Most recipes will tell you to fold with a spatula or metal spoon which works fine, but I really like to use a wire whisk to fold, as almost no air gets knocked out of the mixture.
4. Tell whoever is eating them to sit at the table as the mighty risen soufflé will look great for about 5 minutes, then it will sink down again.
5. When it comes to eating a soufflé, my favourite thing to do is scoop out a little from the centre, eat it, then place a scoop of ice cream in the hole I've just created so it melts through the soufflé. Yum!

MATTY'S PASSIONFRUIT SOUFFLÉ (DECEPTIVELY SIMPLE)

SERVES 2½ (2 SOUFFLÉS PLUS SOME FOR YOU TO EAT OUT OF THE BOWL!)

Who would have thought a soufflé could have so few ingredients? Provided you follow my soufflé tips on the previous pages, I promise you will be as wowed by this soufflé as I was when my mate Matt made these for dessert one night. Fresh passionfruit is best for this recipe; I find the tinned pulp makes it a bit too sweet.

canola spray oil
50 g (1¾ oz) caster (superfine) sugar, plus extra for dusting
3–4 passionfruit
2 free-range eggs, separated

1. Preheat the oven to 190°C (375°F/Gas 5). Grease two 185 ml (6 fl oz/¾ cup) capacity straight-sided ramekins with the spray oil then dust liberally with caster sugar. Turn each ramekin around to make sure the whole inside surface is coated in a thin layer of sugar. Tip out any excess sugar.
2. Cut the passionfruit in half and scoop their pulp into a sieve over a bowl to catch the juices. Measure out 1½ tablespoons of their juice and put it aside. Keep the leftover pulp for your muesli the next day.
3. Put the egg yolks in a large bowl with half the sugar and whisk vigorously until the sugar is completely dissolved. Whisk in the passionfruit juice until combined then set aside.
4. Use hand-held electric beaters to whisk the egg whites in a large bowl with a pinch of salt to soft peaks. Slowly add the remaining caster sugar until firm peaks form. Whisk a third of this meringue mixture into the passionfruit mixture until completely incorporated, then carefully fold in the remaining meringue, trying to retain all that air you beat in.
5. Spoon the soufflé mixture into the ramekins until slightly over-full. Use a knife to smooth the top of each soufflé by running it flat against the top rim of the ramekin.
6. Place the ramekins on a baking tray and bake for 10–15 minutes, or until risen and golden. Serve immediately!

RASPBERRY SOUFFLÉ {SERVES 4}

Get ready to get your soufflé on. This is a great recipe to start with if you haven't made a soufflé before, and using frozen raspberries means it's easy and affordable all year round.

canola spray oil, for greasing
75 g (2¾ oz/⅓ cup) caster (superfine) sugar, plus 2 tablespoons more, and a little extra, for dusting
200 g (7 oz/about 1⅔ cups) frozen raspberries, defrosted
1 heaped teaspoon cornflour (cornstarch)
3 free-range egg whites
vanilla ice cream, to serve (optional)

1. Preheat the oven to 180°C (350°F/Gas 4). Grease four 185 ml (6 fl oz/¾ cup) capacity straight-sided ramekins with the spray oil. Dust liberally with caster sugar and turn each ramekin until you have a thin, even layer of sugar coating the inside. Tip the excess sugar into the next ramekin and repeat.
2. Use a spatula to force the defrosted raspberries through a fine sieve, making sure you force through as much of the pulp as possible. Discard the seeds so you are left with a thick raspberry purée.
3. Combine the 75 g (2¾ oz/⅓ cup) of caster sugar and 2 tablespoons of water in a small saucepan over a low heat and cook until the sugar has completely dissolved.
4. Meanwhile, whisk the cornflour into the raspberry purée until dissolved. Add this raspberry mixture to the saucepan of sugar syrup, whisk carefully to combine, then increase the heat to high and bring to the boil. Whisk for 1 minute, or until slightly thickened then transfer to a large bowl and allow to cool for at least 5 minutes.
5. Whisk your egg whites until soft peaks form, then sprinkle in the 2 tablespoons of sugar while still whisking until firm peaks form. Use a whisk to mix a third of the egg white into the raspberry syrup until well combined. Very carefully, fold in the remaining egg white.
6. Spoon the mixture into the ramekins until slightly over-full, and use a knife to smooth the top of each soufflé, if you like. Place the ramekins on a baking tray and bake for 10–15 minutes, or until risen and slightly golden. Serve immediately with ice cream. Soufflés don't wait for anyone!

TWO NUTELLA CUPCAKES {SERVES 2}

You know those times when you have a hankering for some baked goods, but you don't want to make a whole pile of cakes, or you don't have enough ingredients in the cupboard? Well this is the perfect solution. It's the simplest possible melt 'n' mix cupcake batter, followed by a really quick frosting. Minimal prep time. Minimal washing-up. Maximum cupcake goodness.

CUPCAKES

1 free-range egg white
2 tablespoons of caster (superfine) sugar
30 g (1 oz) unsalted butter, melted
2 tablespoons plain (all-purpose) flour
1 tablespoon unsweetened cocoa powder
¼ heaped teaspoon baking powder
1½ tablespoons milk

NUTELLA FROSTING

25 g (1 oz) unsalted butter, at room temperature
75 g (2¾ oz/¼ cup) Nutella
¼ teaspoon natural vanilla extract
1 tablespoon icing (confectioners') sugar

1. Preheat the oven to 180°C (350°F/Gas 4). Line two holes of a 12-hole standard (80 ml/2½ fl oz/⅓ cup) muffin tin with two paper cupcake cases. In a bowl, whisk the egg white and sugar until combined. Add the melted butter and whisk again until combined then whisk in the flour, cocoa powder, baking powder and a pinch of salt until smooth. Whisk in the milk until the mixture has reached a batter consistency.
2. Divide the batter evenly between the two paper cases. Bake for 15–20 minutes, or until the cakes are rounded on top and coming away from the sides, and a skewer inserted into the centre comes out clean. Move to a wire rack and leave to cool completely.
3. To make the frosting, place the butter and Nutella in the bowl of an electric mixer and beat together until combined and fluffy. Add the vanilla extract and icing sugar and beat again until you've got a nice, smooth spreading consistency.
4. Top the cooled cupcakes with the Nutella frosting and serve.

MUM'S DARK CHOCOLATE & COFFEE TART {SERVES 6–8}

This tart is based on one of Mum's recipes from the tattered old cookbooks that she used to handwrite. They're in rather awful condition, which is usually a sign that you have used those cookbooks a lot and the recipes in them are good! My mum has a serious chocolate addiction, so it's safe to say a good portion of her recipes are exactly like this one: decadent, rich and delicious.

BISCUIT BASE

100 g (3½ oz) unsalted butter, melted, plus extra for greasing
250 g (9 oz) plain chocolate biscuits

FILLING

200 g (7 oz) dark chocolate
125 g (4½ oz) unsalted butter
75 g (2¾ oz/⅓ cup) caster (superfine) sugar
2 tablespoons unsweetened cocoa powder
1 tablespoon instant coffee granules
4 free-range eggs
icing (confectioners') sugar, for dusting

1. Preheat your oven to 180°C (350°F/Gas 4). Grease a 25 cm (10 inch) loose-based tart (flan) tin. Place the biscuits in a food processor and chop until very fine. Tip into a large bowl and mix in the melted butter until combined. Press this biscuit mixture evenly into the tart tin, pressing it right into the edges and up the side. Cover with plastic wrap and refrigerate.
2. Place the chocolate in a heatproof bowl over a saucepan of simmering water (make sure the water isn't touching the bottom of the bowl). Stir until melted and smooth. Once melted, put aside.
3. Use hand-held electric beaters to cream the butter and sugar together with the cocoa powder and instant coffee until smooth and a little fluffy. While the beaters are running, pour in the melted chocolate and continue to mix until combined.
4. Beat the eggs in a separate bowl for 2–3 minutes, or until pale and thickened. Beat in the chocolate mixture until just combined.
5. Remove the tin from the fridge and place onto a baking tray. Pour in the chocolate mixture and jiggle gently to evenly distribute the filling. Bake for 35–40 minutes, or until the filling no longer wobbles when you shake the tin. Remove from the oven and leave to cool.
6. Carefully remove from the tin, dust with a little icing sugar and slice into wedges to serve.

MALVA PUDDING {SERVES 6}

Chloe and I were lucky enough to visit South Africa last year, and we stayed with two lovely locals, Sabrina and Gareth. They took us under their wing and introduced us to all the local must-eats: biltong (cured meat), braii (barbecue) and rusk biscuits dipped in rooibos tea. But hands-down, malva pudding was our favourite; it's a sort of sticky toffee pudding with apricot jam mixed through for flavour. The recipe makes a ridiculous amount of toffee sauce, but I promise you that's how it's supposed to be served.

PUDDING BATTER

30 g (1 oz) unsalted butter, melted, plus extra for greasing
125 ml (4 fl oz/½ cup) milk
1 teaspoon bicarbonate of soda (baking soda)
225 g (8 oz/1½ cups) self-raising flour
75 g (2¾ oz/⅓ cup) caster (superfine) sugar
2 free-range eggs, lightly beaten
85 g (3 oz/¼ cup) apricot jam
thin (pouring) cream or vanilla ice cream, to serve

TOFFEE SAUCE

200 g (7 oz) unsalted butter
250 ml (9 fl oz/1 cup) thickened (whipping) cream
220 g (7¾ oz/1 cup) caster (superfine) sugar
250 ml (9 fl oz/1 cup) water
1 teaspoon vanilla bean paste

1. Preheat the oven to 180°C (350°F/Gas 4). Grease a 2 litre (70 fl oz/8 cup) capacity rectangular pudding dish. Combine the milk and bicarbonate of soda in a bowl and whisk until the bicarb has dissolved. Add the flour, sugar, eggs, jam, melted butter and a pinch of salt, and whisk until combined.
2. Pour the batter into the pudding dish and bake for 20–30 minutes, or until the pudding is golden brown on top.
3. Meanwhile, make the toffee sauce. Place all of the ingredients in a medium–large saucepan over a medium heat, and stir until the butter has melted, the sugar has dissolved and all the ingredients are evenly combined.
4. While the pudding is still hot, use a fork to poke lots of holes in the top, to allow the sauce to seep into the pudding. Slowly pour the sauce all over and leave for a few minutes, so it can cool while the sauce soaks in.
5. Place the pudding in the middle of the table with the cream or vanilla ice cream and let everyone serve themselves.

S'MORE PEANUT BUTTER COOKIES

{MAKES ABOUT 24 COOKIES}

These cookies have all the best bits of a S'more, that classic campfire treat from the US. Gooey marshmallow, melty chocolate and crunchy peanuts, all conveniently bound together in a hand-held treat. When forming the dough balls, do your best to make sure the marshmallows are inside the balls as much as possible. This ensures they'll stay gooey inside the cookie and won't melt all over your tray. Try and stop at just one!

- 75 g (2¾ oz) unsalted butter, plus extra for greasing
- 150 g (5½ oz/½ cup) smooth peanut butter
- 100 g (3½ oz/½ cup, lightly packed) brown sugar
- 110 g (3¾ oz/½ cup) caster (superfine) sugar
- 2 free-range eggs
- 260 g (9¼ oz/1¾ cups) self-raising flour
- ¼ teaspoon salt
- 150 g (5½ oz/¾ cup) chocolate chips
- 30 g (1 oz/⅔ cup) mini marshmallows

1. Lightly grease two large baking trays. Use an electric mixer or hand-held electric beaters to cream the butter, peanut butter and both types of sugar together until pale and creamy (this will take about 2–4 minutes of solid beating).
2. Beat in the eggs, one at a time, until combined. Use a spatula or wooden spoon to mix in the flour and salt until just incorporated. Add the chocolate chips and mini marshmallows and briefly fold them through. Roll up your sleeves and use your hands to make sure the chocolate and marshmallows are evenly distributed. You could probably get away without using your hands, but it's fun and you get to eat some raw cookie dough after, which is half the reason to make cookies!
3. Roll the mixture into balls roughly the size of golf balls and place on the trays, leaving at least 4 cm (1½ inches) between them to allow for spreading.
4. Wrap both trays in plastic wrap and refrigerate for at least 1 hour. Don't skip this step; if you bake these straight from room temperature the cookies won't hold their shape.
5. Preheat the oven to 160°C (315°F/Gas 2–3). Bake the cookies for 10–12 minutes, depending on your oven and whether you want them chewy or crispy. The cookies will still be a bit soft when they come out of the oven; they'll firm up as they cool. Allow to cool a little on the tray, but eat pretty soon after that; these are at their most delicious when they are a little warm and gooey.

ESSENTIALS

SAVOURY ESSENTIALS

These flavour bases are simple and quick to prepare, and I think they should be in every cook's arsenal. In fact, most of these don't require much more than a mixing bowl, a saucepan or a food processor. They are building blocks to a whole pile of great dishes, so I've recommended uses for all of them. I'm sure you'll think of many more.

OLIVE & DRIED FIG TAPENADE

{MAKES ABOUT 1¼ CUPS}

Tapenade makes a great dip or spread. One of my favourite ways to use it is to spread it over a pizza base for a big punch of flavour, then top with things like caramelised onions, thyme and goat's cheese. You can also stuff it in mushrooms, toss it through pasta, or serve it with grilled white fish or lamb.

If you have a food processor, blitz everything, except the extra virgin olive oil, in it until very finely chopped. Add the olive oil then blitz again briefly until just combined. If you don't have a food processor, chop all the ingredients as finely as you can, then add the olive oil and stir to combine.

- 150 g (5½ oz/1 cup) pitted kalamata olives
- 3 dried figs, knobbly tips cut off, flesh roughly chopped
- 1 garlic clove, minced or finely chopped
- 1 tablespoon baby capers, drained and rinsed
- 1 tablespoon balsamic vinegar
- 2 teaspoons finely grated orange zest (optional if you have an orange lying around in your fruit bowl)
- 60 ml (2 fl oz/¼ cup) extra virgin olive oil

HONEY & BALSAMIC GLAZE

{MAKES A LITTLE OVER ¼ CUP}

This is great drizzled over grilled meats or haloumi. It also works nicely as a glaze over roasted salmon or chicken drumsticks. It has a great balance of sweet and sour.

Cook the balsamic vinegar and honey together in a microwave or small saucepan over a medium heat until syrupy.

- 125 ml (4 fl oz/½ cup) balsamic vinegar
- 90 g (3¼ oz/¼ cup) honey

BEST. GUACAMOLE. EVER.

{MAKES ABOUT 1 CUP}

There are two types of guacamole: smooth and chunky. For the first, the trick is to blend the avocado so you have a perfectly smooth dip. For the second, you can deliberately leave everything a bit chunky so you end up with something between a salsa and an avocado salad. Over years (yes, years!) of making guacamole in different ways, I've come to the conclusion that the chunky type is my favourite. It has a great texture that is different with every bite. When you're buying an avocado, make sure it's ripe by gently pressing the top. If it gives slightly, perfect. If it is super squishy or hard as a rock, leave it.

2 spring onions (scallions)
1 tablespoon sliced jalapeño (available in jars in the Mexican section of most supermarkets)
½ a handful of coriander (cilantro) leaves (optional)
1 avocado
juice of ½ a lime

1. Thinly slice the spring onions (whites and greens). Add the jalapeños and coriander leaves (if using) to the chopping board and, using a rocking action with your knife, chop the ingredients together until they resemble a chunky paste. Transfer to a bowl.
2. Carefully, cut the avocado in half around the stone. Put the half with the stone on the chopping board. Use a large knife and with one firm, confident action, chop into the big stone. Gently twist the knife to remove the stone. Carefully knock down on the stone to remove it from the knife. Slice a crosshatch pattern in the avocado flesh before scooping it out of its skin. Add the diced avocado to the spring onion paste.
3. Mash a little of the avocado with a fork, but keep it mostly in chunks. Squeeze over the lime juice and add a big pinch of salt. Stir gently to combine and use straight away. It will keep in the fridge for a few hours, but it's best when you first make it.

TRADITIONAL PESTO {MAKES 2/3 CUP}

Pesto is great on sandwiches, with chicken dishes or stirred through pasta, and it will keep covered in the fridge for three to four days. If you want to get creative, you can add some rocket (arugula) or baby spinach, or swap the basil for coriander (cilantro). The pine nuts can even be swapped with cashews or almonds.

40 g (1½ oz/¼ cup) pine nuts
2 large handfuls of basil leaves
1 small garlic clove, crushed
finely grated zest and juice of ½ a lemon (optional)
60 ml (2 fl oz/¼ cup) extra virgin olive oil
25 g (1 oz/¼ cup) finely grated parmesan cheese

1. Preheat the oven to 180°C (350°F/Gas 4). Sprinkle the pine nuts onto a baking tray and toast them in the oven for 5 minutes, or until lightly golden. Alternatively, you can toast them in a hot, dry frying pan over a medium heat, tossing regularly, for 1–3 minutes, or until lightly golden. Allow to cool.
2. Combine the pine nuts with the basil leaves, garlic and a pinch of salt in the bowl of a food processor and process until finely chopped. Add the lemon zest and juice (if using) and the extra virgin olive oil. Stir until completely combined then stir in the parmesan.

CHILLI CHUTNEY {MAKES 1 CUP}

This sauce packs a punch. You can serve it with rice, noodles or dumplings, add it to a stir-fry, or serve it with pork, prawn (shrimp) or leafy green vegetable dishes. Any sauce you have left over will keep in an airtight container in the fridge for up to a week.

6 large red chillies, seeded
2 shallots, roughly chopped
6 garlic cloves
a matchbox-sized piece of ginger, peeled and roughly chopped
80 ml (2½ fl oz/⅓ cup) vegetable or canola oil
2 teaspoons brown sugar
1 tablespoon soy sauce
1½ teaspoons Chinese black vinegar

1. Combine the chillies, shallot, garlic and ginger in a food processor and blitz until fine (or chop until fine).
2. Heat the vegetable or canola oil in a small heavy-based saucepan over a medium–high heat. Add the chilli mixture and reduce the heat to medium. Cook, stirring often, for 2–4 minutes, or until lightly golden. Add the sugar and soy sauce, turn the heat down to low and cook for a further 8–10 minutes, or until it smells delicious and the oil has separated out a bit.
3. Remove from the heat, stir through the black vinegar and allow to cool.

ROASTED CAPSICUM HUMMUS

{MAKES 2⅔ CUPS}

Serve this vivid red dip alongside pitta bread, or smear it on lamb burgers right before serving.

- 1 x 400 g (14 oz) jar or tin of roasted red capsicums (peppers) (available from the deli section of your supermarket), drained
- 1 x 400 g (14 oz) tin of chickpeas, rinsed and drained
- 2 tablespoons tahini (optional)
- juice of 1 lemon
- 1 tablespoon ground cumin
- 2 teaspoons smoked paprika
- 60 ml (2 fl oz/¼ cup) olive oil

Combine all of the ingredients with a big pinch of salt in a food processor. Blend until smooth.

RED ONION MARMALADE {MAKES 2 CUPS}

This marmalade is absolutely perfect with vegetables, cheese or eggs, so things like frittatas and quiches really benefit from a spoonful. It's also best friends with red meat. Store any leftover marmalade in an airtight container in the fridge for up to two weeks.

- 2 tablespoons olive oil
- 4 red onions, halved and sliced as thinly as possible
- 60 ml (2 fl oz/¼ cup) balsamic or red wine vinegar
- 1½ tablespoons brown sugar
- 3 thyme sprigs, leaves picked (optional)

1. Heat the olive oil in a large heavy-based saucepan or frying pan over a medium heat. Add the sliced onion and cook, stirring occasionally, for 10 minutes, or until the onion has softened.
2. Add the vinegar, sugar and thyme leaves (if using), then season to taste with salt and freshly ground black pepper and cook for a further 10–15 minutes, or until the onion has darkened and the mixture has a jammy consistency.

QUICK PICKLED CUCUMBER

{MAKES 1 CUP}

This is David Chang's method of using salt and sugar to quickly draw moisture out of cucumber so its texture resembles that of a vinegar pickle, which needs to sit for much longer before it can be used. He uses his quick pickle on pork buns, but I love it with seafood or the chilli on page 101.

- 1 Lebanese (short) cucumber, thinly sliced
- 1 tablespoon caster (superfine) sugar
- 1 teaspoon salt
- a handful of coriander (cilantro) leaves, to serve

Combine the cucumber, sugar and salt in a bowl. Set aside for 20 minutes, or until the cucumber has softened then serve as a side dish with a few coriander leaves scattered on top.

A SIMPLE BUT PROPER TZATZIKI

{MAKES 1¼ CUPS}

It's super important that you squeeze as much excess water from the cucumber as possible after you grate it for this tzatziki, so don't skip that step – it's the difference between a moreish dip and a thin, runny, flavourless sauce. It's brilliant on grilled pitta bread, falafel or grilled chicken.

- 1 Lebanese (short) cucumber
- ¼ teaspoon salt
- 200 g (7 oz/¾ cup) thick Greek yoghurt
- 1 small garlic clove, finely grated (optional)
- 2 teaspoons lemon juice
- 2 tablespoons extra virgin olive oil
- 2 teaspoons finely chopped dill (optional)

1. Slice the cucumber in half lengthways, then use a teaspoon to scrape all the seeds out. Discard the seeds. Coarsely grate the cucumber, sprinkle with the salt then squeeze it between two pieces of paper towel to remove as much moisture as possible.
2. Put the squeezed cucumber into a bowl with the yoghurt, garlic (if using), lemon juice, olive oil and dill (if using). Stir to combine then season to taste.

TOMATO & FENNEL MULTIPURPOSE SAUCE {MAKES 2 CUPS}

This sauce has pasta or gnocchi with parmesan written all over it (see page 91). It's also great with meatballs (see page 94), eggplant (aubergine) and seafood; try serving it with penne and flaked tuna for a simple meal. If you've never used fennel seeds in your cooking before, now is the time to try it. Your supermarket will definitely have them, and they'll give your sauce the most amazing aroma and subtle flavour.

- 2 tablespoons olive oil
- 1 brown onion, diced
- 4 garlic cloves, thinly sliced
- 1 long red chilli, seeded and thinly sliced
- 2 teaspoons fennel seeds
- 2 x 400 g (14 oz) tins of chopped tomatoes
- 2 teaspoons caster (superfine) sugar

1. Pour the olive oil into a large heavy-based saucepan over a high heat. Add the onion and garlic and cook until translucent, stirring occasionally.
2. Add the chilli and fennel seeds. Continue to cook until you can smell the fennel seeds and everything is starting to turn golden brown. Add the tomatoes and sugar, and season with salt and freshly ground black pepper. Simmer for 20–25 minutes, or until the sauce has darkened slightly. Use immediately or cool and refrigerate for up to 4 days.

HOISIN DIPPING SAUCE {MAKES 2/3 CUP}

This is so simple it isn't really even a recipe. It's worthy of inclusion, though, as it is so darn tasty with cold Vietnamese rice paper rolls, roasted chicken or stirred through a noodle stir-fry.

- 125 ml (4 fl oz/½ cup) hoisin sauce
- 2 teaspoons light soy sauce
- 2 teaspoons rice wine vinegar
- 1 heaped teaspoon very finely grated fresh ginger

Combine all of the ingredients in a small bowl and stir to combine. Easy.

CHIMICHURRI {MAKES ⅔ CUP}

Think of chimichurri as a sort-of Argentinean pesto. Spoon a generous amount on a steak sandwich (see page 58), or serve it with grilled veggies or haloumi.

a handful of flat-leaf (Italian) parsley leaves
a handful of coriander (cilantro) leaves
2 teaspoons ground cumin
dried chilli flakes, to taste
1 garlic clove, crushed or grated
2 tablespoons red wine vinegar
125 ml (4 fl oz/½ cup) olive oil

1. Combine all of the ingredients, except the olive oil, in a food processor and blend until smooth. For a more rustic chimichurri, skip the processor and just chop everything together with a knife. Once blended, stir in the olive oil.
2. If not using straight away, transfer the chimichurri to a jar or container with a narrow opening. Top with a small amount of olive oil to stop the herbs discolouring too quickly then seal and refrigerate for up to a week.

GREEN NAHM JIM {MAKES ⅓ CUP}

This sauce has a bit of heat to it so don't give it to your four-year-old niece! It's great on all seafood, and with salads containing tropical fruit such as mango (see page 136), lychee or papaya.

2 garlic cloves, peeled
1 long green chilli, seeded
1½ tablespoons fish sauce
2 teaspoons brown sugar
a handful of chopped coriander (cilantro) roots, stems and leaves
juice of 1 lime

Combine all of the ingredients in a food processor or mortar and pestle and blend or pound until smooth.

ESSENTIALS

SWEET ESSENTIALS

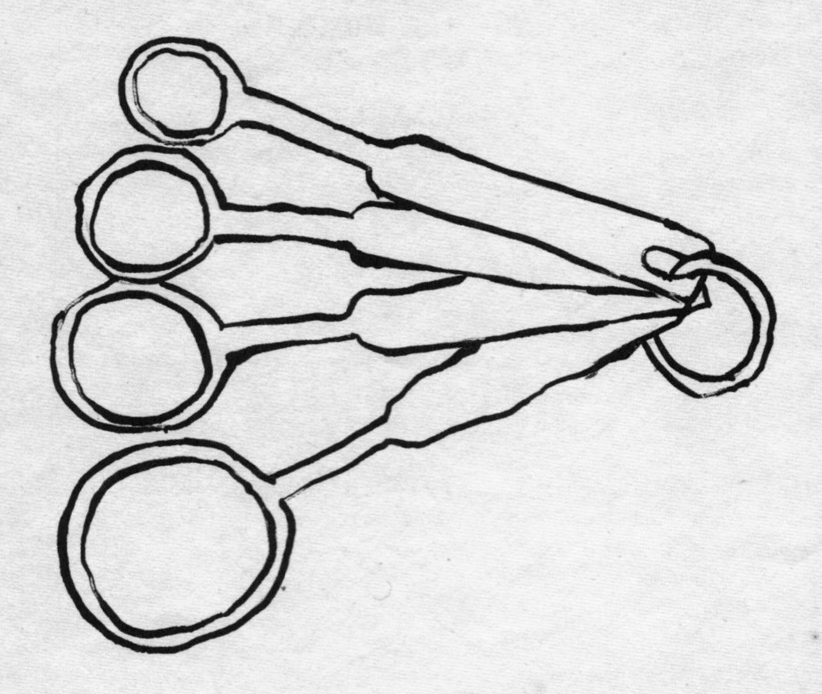

If you want to have a crack at making some desserts, you really need to start with some solid base recipes. This is the one part of the book where straying from the recipe isn't necessarily a good idea, so have your scales and measuring cups at the ready!

CHOCOLATE GANACHE {MAKES 1⅔ CUPS}

Ganache is so versatile. It can be used as a tart filling, served with fruit or beaten a little to create a decadent cake icing.

200 g (7 oz) dark, milk or white chocolate
60 g (2¼ oz) unsalted butter
140 ml (4½ fl oz) thickened (whipping) cream

1. Melt the chocolate and butter in a heatproof bowl over a small saucepan of simmering water (make sure the water is not touching the bottom of the bowl). Gently stir the chocolate with a metal spoon until melted then remove from the heat. Alternatively, you can melt the chocolate in a microwave-safe container in the microwave on full power in 10-seconds bursts, stirring after each burst until smooth.
2. Add one-third of the cream to the melted chocolate and whisk until completely incorporated. Whisk in another third of the cream, then the final third. Allow to cool in the refrigerator, stirring occasionally, until thickened but not set hard.

LEMON CURD {MAKES 1½ CUPS}

Everyone needs to have a recipe for lemon curd and this one is my favourite. Use it as the filler in sandwich biscuits, spoon it into tarts or layer cakes, or serve it with fruit-based desserts.

65 g (2⅓ oz) butter
2½ tablespoons lemon juice
2 free-range eggs
100 g (3½ oz) caster (superfine) sugar

1. Bring the butter and lemon juice to the boil in a small saucepan over a medium–high heat. In a medium bowl, whisk together the eggs and caster sugar until combined.
2. While whisking, pour the boiling butter and lemon juice into the egg mixture, whisking very quickly to combine. Return to a clean saucepan and cook over a medium heat, whisking constantly, until thickened. Remove from the heat. Whisk for another minute or so to cool quickly, then refrigerate for 1–2 hours, until thickened.

SIMPLE CRUMBLE {MAKES ABOUT 1¼ CUPS}

This crumble recipe is best baked on its own in the oven before sprinkling over poached fruit, custard or ice cream. Flavour it with spices such as ginger, nutmeg or cinnamon.

65 g (2⅓ oz) plain (all-purpose) flour
50 g (1¾ oz) unsalted butter
30 g (1 oz) caster (superfine) sugar
½–1 teaspoon ground spice of your choice

1. Preheat the oven to 190°C (375°F/Gas 5) and line a baking tray with baking paper.
2. Blend all of the ingredients together in a food processor with a pinch of salt until the mixture resembles fine breadcrumbs. You could also rub everything together with your fingers in a bowl.
3. Spread the crumbs over the lined tray and bake at for 5–6 minutes, stirring once or twice.

CRÈME PÂTISSIÈRE (OR CRÈME PAT) {MAKES 1⅓ CUPS}

You know that super-thick custard on the inside of a chocolate éclair? That bad boy is crème pâtissière, or 'crème pat'. It's mostly milk thickened with a relatively high amount of cornflour and made glossy and rich with the addition of butter. It's great for layering in trifles, filling tarts or piping into profiteroles.

375 ml (13 fl oz/1½ cups) milk
1 teaspoon vanilla bean paste
5 free-range egg yolks
75 g (2¾ oz/⅓ cup) caster (superfine) sugar
30 g (1 oz/¼ cup) cornflour (cornstarch)
35 g (1¼ oz) unsalted butter

1. Combine the milk and vanilla bean paste in a small saucepan over a high heat. Bring to a simmer then remove from the heat.
2. Meanwhile, whisk the egg yolks, sugar and cornflour together in a large bowl until well combined. Slowly whisk in the vanilla milk until it's all incorporated. Pour the mixture back into the saucepan. Place over a medium heat and whisk until the custard boils and thickens. Remove from the heat. Pour this custard into a bowl, whisk for a minute to cool it a little before whisking in the butter. Refrigerate until ready to use.

BASIC FRANGIPANE

{MAKES 2 CUPS OF FRANGIPANE BATTER}

Frangipane is an almondy tart filling traditionally used in fruit tarts, or baked with liqueurs. The basic recipe for it is below, but I like to add to it sometimes by stuffing it with fruit and baking it by itself for a super-moist cake.

115 g (4 oz) unsalted butter, chopped, at room temperature, plus extra for greasing
115 g (4 oz) icing (confectioners') sugar
115 g (4 oz) almond meal
25 g (1 oz) plain (all-purpose) flour
2 free-range eggs
2 tablespoons liqueur such as Amaretto or Frangelico (optional)
1 cup chopped or sliced fruit, such as apple, pear, berries, pitted cherries, peaches or plums

1. Preheat the oven to 190°C (375°F/Gas 5). Grease and line a 12 × 24 cm (4½ × 9½ inch) loaf (bar) tin. Sift the icing sugar, then the almond meal and flour into a large bowl. Use hand-held electric beaters or an electric stand mixer to beat in the soft butter until just combined. Beat in one of the eggs, and once it is completely combined, beat in the other. If adding a liqueur, stir that in now.
2. Spoon the mixture into the lined tin and level it out a little with a spatula. If you want to add fruit, push pieces of your chosen fruit into the batter now. Bake for 40–45 minutes, or until a skewer inserted into the centre comes out clean. Remove from the oven and cool in the tin. Carefully remove from the tin and slice.

KIRSTY'S CUSTARD {MAKES 2 CUPS}

This is a recipe I stole from my sister years ago — an oldie but a goodie. It's a thin pouring custard that's great with dishes like apple crumble or Christmas pudding.

150 ml (5 fl oz) thickened (double) cream
150 ml (5 fl oz) milk
3 free-range egg yolks
55 g (2 oz/¼ cup) caster (superfine) sugar
2 teaspoons vanilla bean paste
1 teaspoon cornflour (cornstarch)

1. Combine the cream and milk in a medium saucepan. Bring to a simmer over a medium heat then remove from the heat. Meanwhile, whisk the egg yolks, caster sugar, vanilla bean paste and cornflour together in a medium bowl.
2. Pour the hot cream mixture into the egg mixture, whisking to combine as you go. Once combined, pour this mixture back into the saucepan and cook gently over a medium–low heat, whisking constantly, until thickened. Remove from the heat and pour into a serving jug.

BUTTERSCOTCH SAUCE {MAKES 1⅓ CUPS}

This ridiculously indulgent sauce is awesome on grilled pineapple or banana, spooned over vanilla ice cream or poured over sticky puddings.

100 g (3½ oz) unsalted butter
125 ml (4 fl oz/½ cup) thin (pouring) cream
165 g (5¾ oz/¾ cup, firmly packed) brown sugar
a pinch of salt

Combine all of the ingredients in a medium saucepan over a medium heat. Stir occasionally, and once the butter has melted and the sugar has completely dissolved, whack up the heat to high and simmer for 2 minutes, or until thickened and smooth. It will thicken further as it cools, and the sauce can be reheated if necessary. Don't boil the sauce for too long, or it will start to burn, and definitely don't touch or taste it until it has cooled down.

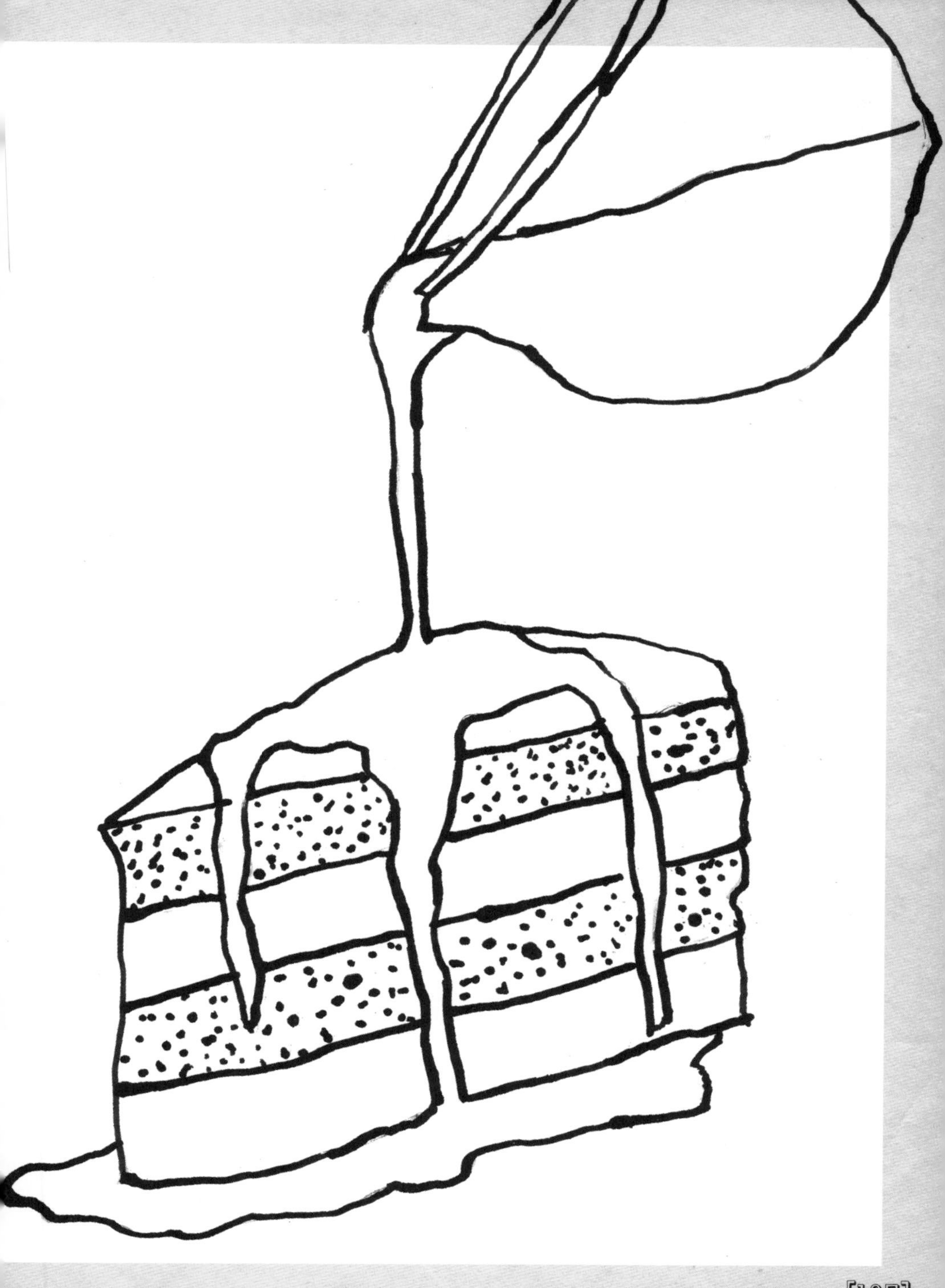

INDEX

Page numbers in *italics* refer to photographs.

ACKNOWLEDGEMENTS

Books don't just happen, and while I'm lucky enough to have my name printed on the cover, there's a whole host of people who deserve to share the credit.

Hugh is responsible for the amazing illustrations and layout of the book, Alan used his photography skills to make the recipes look their Sunday best, and Grace was the glue that held the shoot together.

Sue, Diana, Livia and Katie did plenty of hard work behind the scenes to bring this book to your hands, and had enough faith in me to let me write it.

Lisa, Caitlin and the One Management team continue to work hard to help me live my dreams (namely, being a cookbook author!).

Themis and the Sprout team have worked hard to not only help come up with recipes, but to teach them to other people, which I think is a pretty special gift.

My family and friends are a constant supply of inspiration. Mum and Kirsty give me support, love and recipes. The Gravestock family are some of the nicest people you are likely to meet, and it's awesome to have their help. Chloe gave me some of my favourite recipes, and put in a buttload of hard work to help me write the book. Kyle, Matty, Adam, Dan and Rob all have recipes attributed to them because they are all great cooks in their own right, and fine gentlemen as well.

Dad was a role model for me to get into the kitchen, and for that, I'll be forever grateful.

/callumthann

@callumskitchen

www.callumhann.com.au
www.sproutcooking.com.au

Published in 2014 by Murdoch Books, an imprint of Allen & Unwin.

Murdoch Books Australia
83 Alexander Street
Crows Nest NSW 2065
Phone: +61 (0) 2 8425 0100
Fax: +61 (0) 2 9906 2218
www.murdochbooks.com.au
info@murdochbooks.com.au

Murdoch Books UK
Erico House, 6th Floor
93–99 Upper Richmond Road
Putney, London SW15 2TG
Phone: +44 (0) 20 8785 5995
Fax: +44 (0) 20 8785 5985
www.murdochbooks.co.uk
info@murdochbooks.co.uk

For Corporate Orders & Custom Publishing contact
Noel Hammond, National Business Development Manager, Murdoch Books Australia

Publisher: Diana Hill
Photographer: Alan Benson
Styling, illustrations and design: Hugh Ford
Editor: Katie Bosher
Home economist on shoot: Grace Campbell
Editorial manager: Livia Caiazzo
Production manager: Karen Small

A cataloguing-in-publication entry is available from the catalogue of the National Library of Australia at www.nla.gov.au.

A catalogue record for this book is available from the British Library.

Colour reproduction by Splitting Image, Clayton, Victoria.

Printed by Hang Tai Printing Company.

IMPORTANT: Those who might be at risk from the effects of salmonella poisoning (the elderly, pregnant women, young children and those suffering from immune deficiency diseases) should consult their doctor with any concerns about eating raw eggs.

OVEN GUIDE: You may find cooking times vary depending on the oven you are using. We have used a conventional oven in these recipes, and specified fan-forced in the few recipes that require fan-forced oven. As a general rule, set the temperature for a fan-forced oven 20°C (35°F) lower than indicated in the recipe (unless fan-forced has been specified in the recipe).

MEASURES GUIDE: We have used 20 ml (4 teaspoon) tablespoon measures. If you are using a 15 ml (3 teaspoon) tablespoon add an extra teaspoon of the ingredient for each tablespoon specified.